Storm

from

Paradise

Storm
from
Paradise

The Politics
of Jewish Memory

Jonathan Boyarin

University of Minnesota Press

Minneapolis

Published by the University of Minnesota Press
2037 University Avenue Southeast, Minneapolis, MN 55414
Printed in the United States of America on acid-free paper

Library of Congress Cataloging-in-Publication Data

Boyarin, Jonathan.
  Storm from paradise : the politics of Jewish memory / Jonathan Boyarin.
    p. cm.
  Includes bibliographical references (p.   ) and index.
  ISBN 0-8166-2094-6 (alk. paper). — ISBN 0-8166-2095-4 (alk. paper)
    1. Jews—Identity.   2. Jews—Intellectual life.   3. Judaism—20th century.
  4. Holocaust, Jewish (1939-1945)—Influence.   I. Title.
DS143.B79   1992
305.8'924—dc20   91-34687
                                         CIP

The University of Minnesota is an
equal-opportunity educator and employer.

For Aaron, the brother whom I never knew

With thanks to Uzo, Clint, Glyne, Katy, and Sabine, at the
School of Criticism and Theory, 1988; to my brother, Daniel; to
my sister, Janet; to my father, Sidney; to the Center for Studies
of Social Change, New School for Social Research; and to the
Social Science Research Council/MacArthur Foundation Program in
International Peace and Security

Everything what you know you gotta use.
Moish Fogel, vice president of the Eighth Street Shul

You must remember that Castile is Castile only because of the Indians.
Guaman Poma, cited by Rolena Adorno (1986)

Fight, fight, nigger and a white! Come on, nigger, beat that white!
A chant addressed to the underdog in my preadolescent boys' world;
sometimes I was the "nigger"; I refused to fight.

*He [Rabbi Elazar HaKappar] used to say: the newborn will die; the dead
will live again; the living will be judged—in order that they know, teach,
and become aware that He is God, He is the Fashioner, He is the Creator,
He is the Discerner, He is the Judge, He is the Witness, He is the Plaintiff,
He will judge. Blessed is He, before Whom there is no iniquity, no
forgetfulness, no favoritism, and no acceptance of bribery, for everything is
His. Know that everything is according to the reckoning. And let not your
evil inclination promise you that the grave will be an escape for you—for
against your will were you created; against your will you were born; against
your will you live; against your will you die, and against your will you are
destined to give an account before the King Who rules over Kings,
the Holy One, Blessed is He.*
Ethics of the Fathers, chapter 5

"Charlotte, we're Jewish."
From the film *Mermaids*

Contents

Introduction

I have relied on fragments, bits and pieces of information found here and
there. Sweet late night calls to mama to see if she "remembers when."
Memories of old conversations coming back again and again, memories like
reused fabric in a crazy quilt, contained and kept for the right moment.
I have gathered and remembered. . . . My favorite quilts were those for
everyday use. I was especially fond of the work associated with my mother's
girlhood. When given a choice of quilts, I selected one made of cotton
dresses in cool deep pastels. Baba could not understand when I chose that
pieced fabric of little stars made from my mother's and sister's cotton dresses
over more fancy quilts. Yet those bits and pieces of mama's life,
held and contained there, remain precious to me.

bell hooks (1990: 115-20)

Like the writer who holds on to the scraps of her mother's life and
who has borrowed her great-grandmother's name as her signature, I
share the sense that my own identity is an unstable patchwork of
crosscutting and often contradictory associations. Yet, like almost everyone else, I always act as though I were in fact a subject—a stable
human unit defined in space and time. My work consists of knitting
together patches without obliterating seams. This book, therefore,
considers some relations among three cultural worlds that are central
to my idea of myself: Jewish practice, anthropological fieldwork and
writing, and recent ideas about how to be human at the end of the
twentieth century.

I do mean Jewish *practice*, and not some abstract unity called the
Jewish religion. Jewishness is both a situation into which I was placed
and a choice I make every day when I wake up early to go to the synagogue. The story I tell sometimes about why I started going to the
synagogue every day may help explain the link between the given and
the chosen in my Jewishness.

One night early in 1983, while I was doing fieldwork with Polish
Jewish immigrants in Paris, I had a dream that stayed with me when I
awoke. In the dream I stood in a pine forest next to the lake in Lakewood, New Jersey, where I had spent many summer afternoons in my
childhood. With me was my friend Ralph, a child of survivors whose

knowledge of Yiddish always fascinated me. Around us were Orthodox Jews dressed in black, whom I took to be Lubavitcher Hasidim,
even though most of the Orthodox Jews in Lakewood are actually attached to the non-Hasidic yeshiva there. Suddenly an older woman
approached me, there in the pine grove. Although I had never met her,
I knew that she was from the family that runs the Telz (Telshe) Yeshiva, now in Ohio, which is the family of my mother's father; and I
knew that she was a cousin, one of those who had survived the war
and come to America, whom my mother had once met and spoken of
warmly. This woman spoke to me warmly now, saying, "I just want
you to know, if you ever come to visit us at Telz, you'll be more than
welcome." At that, still in the dream, I burst into tears. Then I immediately awoke, aware of an extremely sore throat. My first thought
was that, if I ever did get to the yeshiva in Cleveland, I would start
putting on *tefillin* ("phylacteries," they're supposed to be called in English, though no one knows what phylacteries are) and praying every
morning.

In the middle of 1983, my wife, Elissa, and I returned to New
York, and late in November I attended an anthropology convention in
Chicago. I decided it was time to visit Telz. But I hadn't put on *tefillin*
since my bar-mitzvah, so two weeks before my trip I found a synagogue with a kind rabbi who taught me once again how to arrange the
leather straps on my head and my right arm. The actual visit to the
Telz Yeshiva is another story, one that I will skip except to say that I
did meet my mother's cousin Rebetzin Chaya Ausband, and she was
every bit as hospitable and impressive a woman as my mother had remembered. The more lasting outcome of this sequence of events—
fieldwork, dream, convention, visit to Telz—has been my continued
attendance at Rabbi Singer's morning services on the Lower East Side
of New York City, an anchor in everyday Jewish community that
complicates my radical activism and critical theory.

My involvement in the Lower East Side Orthodox community also
enabled me to continue doing ethnography without any institutional
support (see J. Boyarin 1988, 1989, 1990), even though I only gradually came to see that involvement as "fieldwork." Nor was the dream
about Telz divorced from the fieldwork I had been doing in Paris. If it
helped clarify a direction in my life, the message it brought was not a
mystical one. Rather it was a poetic correlative of a critical insight,

based on my fieldwork among the last generation of Yiddish secular-
ists, that the continuity of Jewish identity must be grounded in some
form of distinctive everyday practice. The tradition of fieldwork, with
its need to articulate and sustain a double consciousness, has helped me
to continue that practice without convincing myself that I am more of
a believer than I could ever possibly be.

As in much feminist anthropology, then, ethnography for me is
a practice that grows out of the material conditions of my life (see
Mascia-Lees, Sharpe, and Cohen 1989). How I became an ethnographer
of Jews is a story I have written elsewhere (J. Boyarin 1988), but there
are a few moments in that story that have a bearing on the critical
themes I develop in this book. The first is a pivotal break between the
declining Jewish chicken-farm community of Farmingdale, New Jersey, which my family left when I was ten years old, and the nearby
segregated suburb where I lived until I left for college. That move has
acquired in retrospect an ontological status; it represents a change in
my sense of *being* in the world, the moment when the world was set
outside of me as something apart. Childhood in Farmingdale—where
I heard Yiddish every day, built play forts with poor black friends, had
living grandparents, lived more in the kitchen than the living room—
came to represent for me an unfractured primitive world, a golden
age, a *shtetl*, even as I came to know that all three of these were fictions. By contrast, the cold Judaism of the suburb was something that,
in good adolescent conscience, I could only regretfully reject—until I
went to college on the West Coast and was shocked at how little social
resonance I felt once I was removed from an everyday Jewish community, no matter how weak that community was. I call those years at
Reed College the time of the origin of negative identification. It was
the time when I decided that, no matter how shallow everyday Judaism in America seemed to be, I had been shaped more than I could
know by being born into a Jewish history. I decided that my best
course would be to embrace that history, to choose out of the store-
house of everything called Jewish that which could enable me to grow
into an autonomous adult.

How successful I've been is not for me to judge, and probably not
the point. In any case, I never expected to reach a final, stable identity.
That's another reason why I like to refer to myself, half-jokingly, as a
"practicing" Jew: I don't think I'll ever get it entirely right. Nor do I

mean, by this bit of autobiography, to establish my credentials for
speaking "as a Jew," and certainly not *for* other Jews. But given the
rarefied critical air of much of this book, a story or two seemed necessary at the beginning to counter the tendency toward dehistoricized,
disembodied references to Jews in theoretical writing. Especially when
reading French theory, it is not always possible for a reader to distinguish when the literary deployment of "the Jew" represents a conve-
niently dramatic and engagé trope for primarily objectivist categories,
and when it signals an interrogation of the implications of recent history for intellectual categories.[1] My insistence on my living Jewish
voice is intended both to assert that the Jew is more than just "the suffering allegory" (see chapter 4), and also to help guard me against an
objectivized arrogation of the female or postcolonial other in my own
theory building. When I engage those tropes or those voices, it is always on the basis of my own story, which I try to tell as soundly as
I can.[2]

At the same time, I neither can nor want to insist on my Jewish
identity *against* theory. My engagement with theory is no more subordinate to the project of making myself as a Jew than is my practice of
fieldwork and ethnography. It should be obvious that Jews have a special relationship to World War II as a world-defining break, a break
that sets a term not only to anything that could conceivably be
thought of as a basically static "tradition," but to the hopes of modernity as well. Thus Jewish culture and identity have an especially acute
relationship to the problematics of postmodernism, manifested in my
work by the theoretical problems I had to face in trying to use the
tools of modern anthropology to study a destroyed world. Rather
than exploring the varieties of human expression through seeking
face-to-face contact with some ultimate Other, I was deliberately trying to construct myself through contact with my own destroyed "ancestors," the Yiddish-speaking Jews of Eastern Europe (see chapter 5).

That contact could only take place through the mediation of the
books those people had written about their lives (Kugelmass and Boyarin 1983). Those accounts—memorial books written by surviving
Polish Jews about their communities before and during the Nazi
torment—might have been seen as tainted by subjectivism or reified as
first-hand, eyewitness representations. Instead my fellow researcher
and I came to see them as products of the culture of survivors, which

had their own validity, neither one-sidedly "subjective" nor unproblematically "realist," both for the survivors and for those of us who came after (Kugelmass and Boyarin 1988). This exploration of a body of writing in its historical and cultural context eventually helped guide me toward the field of research and criticism now known as cultural studies. Cultural studies overcomes the dichotomy between the study of literature (a tradition with which "we" identify) and the writing of ethnography, the analysis of the distanced Other. It brings the culture of imperial elites and the cultures of those marginalized by world-systemic domination (the majority of humanity) within the same power-laden field. For the critical student of Jewish life, cultural studies offers a way out of the schizoid disciplinary dilemma of trying to squeeze the Jews into definition as a historical or a cultural people, a literary or anthropological phenomenon. Writing theory out of a primary interest in Jewish life in turn offers an opportunity to uncover unsuspected links among knowledge, culture, and power.

The link that I have had to consider in the most sustained way has been the power of the past in the present. Starting with a deep nostalgia for a world that has disappeared, working through the perplexity of being given the tools of ethnographic presence to explore that world, I have come to see through the rhetoric that insists that the past is dead and gone. For me, past and present, like Third World and First, are parts of the same plane linked by multidirectional forces rather than points on a line moving in a single direction of "progress."

This book, then, consists largely of attempts to apply the force of the Jewish past to the dreams of autonomous humanity of Jews and others in the present. My chief guide here is Walter Benjamin, who articulated an ethical messianism, a notion of a time when the memory of all the dreams and suffering of human history would be simultaneously available to each of us. No, he was not really a mystic either: the ideal was heuristic rather than visionary. It was the most potent way he could express his sense that humanity was perpetually betrayed by the oblivious ethic of progress, whether in its Fascist or socialist varieties. What Benjamin perhaps did not realize was that the origin of the idea of triumphal progress was intimately linked to the early church fathers' idea of the progression from Judaism to Christianity (Hanning 1966). Hence Benjamin's critique of progress is linked, more directly than even he could tell us, to the politics of Jewish memory in the twentieth century and before.

My title is drawn from an image of Benjamin's that critics have not tired of citing:

> A Klee painting named 'Angelus Novus' shows an angel
> looking as though he is about to move away from something
> he is fixedly contemplating. His eyes are staring, his mouth is
> open, his wings are spread. This is how one pictures the angel
> of history. His face is turned toward the past. Where we
> perceive a chain of events, he sees one single catastrophe
> which keeps piling wreckage upon wreckage and hurls it in
> front of his feet. The angel would like to stay, awaken the
> dead, and make whole what has been smashed. But a storm is
> blowing from Paradise; it has got caught in his wings with
> such violence that the angel can no longer close them. This
> storm irresistibly propels him into the future to which his
> back is turned, while the pile of debris before him grows
> skyward. This storm is what we call progress. (Benjamin
> 1969b: 257-58)

Most commentators focus, as I have in the past, on the image of history as a continuing catastrophe. But here I want to emphasize the storm still blowing. The eviction of Adam and Eve, like all of the past, is not a one-time event that occurred at what Watergate defendants would call a point in time. Part of the import of Benjamin's image is the lesson that we are always once again being driven out; in some sense we have always just lost paradise, hence we are always close to it. The ongoing state of emergency Benjamin also speaks of doesn't just mean that we are always in imminent danger, but also that something precious is eternally being lost.

This reading of the storm from paradise, which emphasizes both the howling gap between us and the past and the past's proximity to us, suggests the need for a "double gesture" toward our past. We need constantly to be interrogating and recuperating the past, without pretending for long that we can recoup its plenitude.[3] This double gesture, this contradictory movement of new recognitions and new distances between the present and the past, may be most easily articulated in a juxtaposition of explicit traditional and postmodern figures of multiplicity, rather than modern identity. Thus the great eleventh-century Bible commentator Rashi, citing the Babylonian Talmud, likens the various interpretations offered by the rabbis for a single biblical verse to the sparks that fly when a hammer is struck upon a rock (Glatzer 1962). Centuries later, within our lifetime, the Soviet Yiddish poet Peretz Markish described himself, after being disabused of his Stalinist faith, as "a mirror on a stone" (1964: 489). Both images relate in certain ways to the problem of authoritatively grounding ethnic identity in the absence of territorial state power. Yet while Rashi's image of multiplicity suggests complementary abundance, Markish's suggests the fragmentation of the contemporary historical self, its component parts crazily reflecting one another. Today we cannot live only with that disillusion, we who never saw ourselves as the mirror of a fearless leader, nor can we simply reassert Rashi's bedrock of revealed Torah, that solid fount of plural meaning. But we need to refer to both, for least of all can we rely on the self-propelling Progress of Man as the measure of all things.

But there is something that gives us courage in the ability to see unexpected links such as that between Rashi and Markish. We are reaching the limits of a period of nation building when the most important collective was that of contemporaneous individuals defined by their presence within a contiguous space (Anderson 1983). For Jews, that modern notion of solidarity through coterritorial (and in this case, but not all cases, monoethnic) presence has been expressed in Zionism. Postmodern sensibilities allow us to recuperate the alternative (and in this sense traditional) resource of identifying with Jews as a collective through continuity (coextension in time) at least as much as through contiguity (coextension in space). Jews have always, it seems, used narrative to recreate their shared identities across time. This technique demonstrates language as an ethnic strategy that need not impinge upon the autonomy of others. Yet this self-creation of the Jewish collective may also take mythifying forms that endanger the well-being of a contemporary Jewish generation. Thus it is vitally important to consider, for example, Rashi and Markish together, while simultaneously asking whether there is anything unique about *Jewish* panchrony, Jewish collective identification through time, that would permit an identification of Rashi's image with Markish's beyond the point that the premodern and the postmodern are curiously linked. I'm not looking for an answer to that particular question, however; I want neither to dispel the privileged linking of Rashi and Markish as "Jewish thinkers" nor to fix that link. The point of this book is not to identify patterns that are intrinsically or uniquely Jewish, but to find patterns that are "authentically" Jewish and also susceptible to articulation with other "authentic" discourses of memory, resistance, and libera- tion.

The standard way to promote interethnic empathy and solidarity is through the rhetoric of kinship. The family is a powerful image be- cause it refers to something presumed to be a shared value of all ordi- nary people, while allegiance to the circles widening out from our *par- ticular* families also explains our primary loyalty to "our own" people. Yet feminism, in particular, has taught us to be wary of the repressions as well as the connections implicit in the rhetoric of family. And the more mobile we get (and how many of us are willing to sacrifice that mobility?), the less adequate the image of everyday, extended family becomes to our daily realities. The search for "concrete" cultural uni- versals such as the retention of kinship has therefore been destabilized, and needs to be destabilized further (Shell 1988). This does not obviate the possibility of identification through strategic cultural linkages that are chronotopically specific—that is, neither generalized nor eternalized.

An example of this last technique opens Eric Cheyfitz's book on *The Poetics of Imperialism*. The scholar describes a moment in his youth when the mother of his black girlfriend finally asks him whether he is Jewish, and on finding her guess confirmed, says, "I knew you weren't white" (1990: xii). Cheyfitz apparently treasures this memory, as I certainly would, and writes a few more paragraphs about the par- allels among the exclusion of Jews, Native Americans, and African- Americans from elite society. But soon he admits that he will say nothing more of Jews, except to note that "in relation to the Palestin- ians, the Jews . . . find themselves, though not univocally, in the im- perial position of the 'First World' that is the object of my critique in this book" (ibid.: xii-xiv)—an important affirmation as far as it goes. In this book, I am searching for more strategic articulations among Jews and other Others, beyond nostalgia for a lost black-Jewish inti- macy and the recognition that Jews in power need to be criticized as such. In some of these essays (especially "Europe's Indian, America's

Jew"), I'm trying to work through what Cheyfitz calls "the difficult politics of translation."

Perhaps some of my translations will approach the power of the Palestinian lawyer Raja Shehadeh's journal of life under Israeli occupation. In its English edition it was called *The Third Way*, and the cover explained that the title was taken from a saying attributed to Jewish concentration camp inmates: When faced with two alternatives, always choose the third way.

But the American publishers of Shehadeh's book chose yet another way, calling it *Samed* (Shehadeh 1984), the Arabic word expressing the Palestinians' ideal of steadfast refusal to cede their land. The contrast between the two titles, both valid and powerful, suggests another possibility alongside the strategy of contingent linkages, that of

> a philosophical solidarity or community not modeled on
> mutual identification with an ideal or essence, or an agreement
> as to procedure, but which would be brought together by
> what is problematic, unacceptable, intolerable in what we say
> and do to one another, and with the possibilities of saying and
> doing otherwise. (Rajchman 1989: 97)

Most generally, what I find "unacceptable" in cultural studies is the suppression of an autonomous Jewish voice, no matter where that suppression may come from. That suppression should be a concern not only to Jews, for it leaves larger blind spots—some of which I hope to expose in these pages—in the articulation of theory and history, thus pointing as well to some unexpected "possibilities of saying and doing otherwise."

In a project like this, there are bound to be gaps in my reading, unexamined chauvinisms, passages where few will hear the echos of the many meanings *I* thought I was packing inside. Like my idea of practicing Judaism, the book represents ideas arrested at a certain stage of enunciation, not a finished formulation. Likewise, the extreme contemporaneity of the bulk of my critical references is the book's weakness and its strength. For the most part, I am responding to an intellectual ferment around me, not presenting the results of an archaeology of knowledge (although I try to acknowledge some recent cultural studies of the Jew as Europe's Other, among them Shell 1991, Gilman 1986, and Vidal-Nacquet 1982).[4] One consequence is that I inevitably raise vastly more questions than I can even begin to answer.

A few words about the sequence of chapters in this book. I begin with a chapter about forgetting on the Lower East Side, in order to locate myself and simultaneously demystify that "location." I continue with a comparison of two novels, one by a Native American and one by a French Jew, in order to further the themes of resistance to forgetting within a spatially defined cultural space. The chapter on Walter Benjamin and Polish Jews in Paris focuses more closely on the architecture of memory, on the procession of dreams and experiences in the same place over the course of a century. "Jewish Ethnography and the Question of the Book" is closely connected to "The Other Within and the Other Without," since both explore the links between the construction of academic anthropology and the constraints of contemporary Jewish identity. These in turn lead to "The Impossible International," my broadest attempt to articulate postgenocidal Jewishness with feminist and postcolonial politics and theory. Finally, "Palestine and Jewish History" directly confronts the politics of memory with Jews in a position of state power. Throughout the book, I try to complicate the relation between space and time as they constitute memory and identity, against the Cartesian tendency to represent space and time along polar axes.

Finally, I want to acknowledge that the politics of memory is also a much more everyday thing than one would guess from reading this book. What we remember to do, the way we remember things happening, is not only an academic exercise but integral to the persistence of hegemony and resistance in much more prosaic forms than most of the examples I'm dealing with here. I have written what I can for now. It's time for me to put on my *tefillin*.

One

The Lower East Side
A Place of Forgetting

Memory—the free-association counterpart of forgetting—has become associated prominently in our era not only with time, but with space as well.[1] In countries such as France and Israel, the link of memory and space is closely connected to the reinforcement of national identity, a process in which the ideological constructions of uniquely shared land, language, and memory become props for the threatened integrity of the nation-state.

On the other hand, the idea of identifying forgetting with or "in" a certain place would seem to be paradoxical. If memory and forgetting were terms representing simple opposites (such as *plenty* and *famine*), this should not be so. If that were the case, a place or a person should be describable in terms of inverse proportions of memory and forgetting. In fact, the relation is closer to that of direct proportion: it is only by having an inkling of at least the *possible* scope of memory that we can sense the "quantity" of forgetting.[2] Memory and forgetting do seem somehow incommensurate categories; but the reason for this is not to be found in a facile positivist reassurance that the former represents a presence and the latter an absence. Forgetting seems ghostly, not because it has no force or weight (it presses against us heavily and constantly, and it may yet do us in), but because we are so unused to naming it that even those of us who realize its danger usually prefer to speak *for memory*.

The weight of forgetting, then, certainly can be sensed in a certain place — or perhaps we should borrow Bakhtin's term and say in a certain chronotope, a time-place (Bakhtin 1981). My concern here will be the ways that forgetting can be localized and the various forms it takes in a given chronotope — the Jewish Lower East Side of New York City, the paradigmatic Jewish immigrant neighborhood in the New World. While my primary concern is particular rather than comparative, this location is indeed a fit site for a discussion of forgetting: arguably, more has been forgotten in and about the Jewish Lower East Side than virtually any other place or time in America.

I have denied the identification of forgetting with absence without troubling to justify that denial beyond associating the identification with a presumably discredited positivism. More needs to be said about the relation of these two concepts. Since the commonsense (as opposed to Derridean) meaning of *absence* implies spatial nonpresence, a priori one would expect a discussion of a place to speak of absence rather than forgetting. In fact, this spatial absence is linked closely to forgetting, as I will show in the next paragraph. But in the contemporary philosophical interrogation of self, language, and world, absence is a given of consciousness, part and parcel of the separation of ego that defines human existence, as Edmond Jabès's Everyman, Yukel Serafi, says: "I, absent from myself" (Jabès 1977: 236). Absence, like "the individual," that impossible philosophical abstract, exists outside history. Forgetting, on the other hand, is social and historical, and viciously so. It is a given of domination.[3] When Walter Benjamin's angel of history stares backward in horror at a mounting heap of rubble, what he perceives is certainly forgetting, not absence.

The national ideologies I referred to, which employ spatially linked memory to reinforce their own legitimation, are curiously tied to the feudal peasant societies that dissolved and gave way to modern nationalism (Anderson 1983: 17–49). There is a link between the agriculturalist emphasis of early Zionism and the emphasis, in French tourist promotions, on the beauty of the French countryside and the richness of French produce. That link is the image of a people *stable and secure on its own land*. In that image, absence in the everyday sense of being "away from home" is obviously canceled out. Less obviously, the image also promises immunity from forgetting, through the assurance of a generational continuity of memory "rooted" in the soil and of a piece with the life cycle of plants and animals.[4] Tocqueville understood this well and used it in characterizing "traditional" societies: "Families stay in the same situation, and frequently in the same place, for centuries. This, so to speak, renders all the generations contemporary" (cited in Lefort 1986: 303).

For the Jews, however, one must go back much further than the ancien régime in order to find even a convincing image of such a naturally consistent transmission of space and memory.[5] On the contrary, rediasporization is a characteristic pattern of Jewish history that has powerfully shaped Jewish culture.[6] Regarding political Zionism it may be said that the thrust was not so much to overcome the original Exile as to put an end to exiles.

This desire of the Zionists to find a place where the Jews could stay put provides an ironic contrast to the steady decline of the Lower East Side as a Jewish neighborhood, beginning in the 1920s. Of course the living conditions, as in any immigrant ghetto, were terrible, and thus the usual sociological and popular valuation of the neighborhood's depopulation by Jews as upward mobility seems so transparently obvious as not to require explanation. In such a valuation, immigrant misery in turn is implicitly seen as natural, not an aspect of domination. The dispersion and disruption of social networks—such as synagogues built by émigrés from the same hometown (J. Boyarin 1988)—is viewed as a regrettable but affordable consequence of integration into the American system of mobile opportunity. The romantic conception of the restless loner masks the centrality of population transfers in the peculiar dynamic of American capitalism. Mourning for lost common places is suppressed by the constantly reinforced shame of origins,[7] which is complemented, not overcome, by sentimental nostalgia.

A second consideration of the relation of forgetting to space is revealed when we gloss *forgetting* into French as *oubli*, for the French term *oubli* combines two terms that are separated in English, *forgetting* and *oblivion*. While forgetting is a process, an act, oblivion is a state, to which, as we say in English, a particular phenomenon may be consigned. In a somewhat analogous way, space is both a static, existential fact (inasmuch as we cannot exist outside space), and a phenomenon that is shaped dynamically and socially. Between forgetting and oblivion, space as stasis and space as manipulable, there are several possible modalities in which the relation of space to *oubli* can be realized. I have identified three such modalities, but I intend no taxonomy thereby.

The first modality is naked absence. By this I mean the disappearance "without a trace" of landmarks and other foci of ethnic culture. Thus one of the neighborhood's Jewish bookstores was forced to close when the building was sold, shrinking the neighborhood's intellectual resources. There are even more mundane losses; at least four kosher butchers have closed their doors on the Lower East Side in the past decade. Perhaps most violent of all is the removal of portions of the street grid in the process of "urban renewal." I became aware of this last effect when one of the elderly ladies who take the sun in front of my building told me that she used to donate money regularly to "the yeshiva on First Street." I didn't know what she was referring to. I later found out that not only was the yeshiva closed and its building long since demolished, the block on which it once stood no longer exists either.

A second relevant form of forgetting or *oubli* is the reconstruction of a geography of common reference. This is manifest today not on the Lower East Side, but rather in the thriving Hasidic neighborhoods of Brooklyn and the New York suburbs, where rabbinical leaders and the families of those loyal to them are identified according to the names of places in Eastern Europe. Thus Satmar in Hungary, Lubavitch in Lithuania, and Bobov in Poland are all within walking distance of each other in Brooklyn. Yet while the names are perpetuated, the constituencies of the various *rebes* (leaders of particular Hasidic groups) are seldom descended from those who were followers of the *rebe*'s predecessors. The continuity of place names, that is, masks the struggle of the *rebes* and their bands of surviving followers to reassemble a new constituency in post-Holocaust America. Forgetting and memory are so intermingled as to become almost one here. The point is not to separate them, but to realize the surprising point that forgetting is also sometimes a technique of the dominated, used to enable memory.[8]

A third modality creates a representation, a sign to mark simultaneously forgetting and memory. The clearest example of this on the Lower East Side is the facade of a former synagogue, now used as an artist's studio. Evidently the synagogue once had a large, round window, whose panes were separated by pieces of wood in the shape of a Jewish star. Those pieces have now been rearranged into a sort of running pattern around the circumference of the window. To the observer sufficiently sensitized to apprehend the building's former use, the rearranged panels clearly convey a message: *this was and no longer is.* It is almost as if the artist, like some primitive hunter addressing his dead prey, were placating the spirit of the synagogue and its congregation. It hurts. It feels right.

The fact that conventional delimitations of space entail collective representations implies a measure of identification among those who live within or whose ancestors have lived within a given space.[9] The degree to which this identification fails to ground active empathy is another litmus test for the presence of forgetting. The test, of course, does not measure the level of care or thoughtfulness among different individuals; but it does suggest differential relations to space, memory, and forgetting among those conventionally classed together as Jews. The most critical distinction in this regard is between those who still live on the Lower East Side and those who associate with it through memories, symbolic representations (photographs, books, films), or occasional visits.

The present Jewish population of the neighborhood represents itself to outside authorities, such as the city government, through an umbrella group called the United Jewish Council. The council holds an annual dinner around the time of Hanukkah. One year the dinner honored a local rabbi who has invested much energy in working with poor Jews in the neighborhood. He had told several men who couldn't pay the charge for tickets that if they came on the evening of the dinner, places would be found for them. When they arrived, the officer of the United Jewish Council at the door said, "I'll let them in, but not until we arrange seats for them." Eventually they gave up and left. They were forgotten: the polity's most formal manifestation was also most lacking in empathy.

Another anecdote reveals that forgetting is a relative thing. Two years ago my wife, Elissa, and I visited a synagogue in the neighborhood with a young Jewish couple who were visiting from Warsaw. The rabbi was amazed to find out that our friends were planning to return to Poland: "But there's nothing left there!" Elissa asked him how he would respond to a Jew from California who said the same thing about the Lower East Side. He protested: "But it's not true! We still have lots of synagogues here, we still have plenty of Jews here!" He was unable to see that a flame might still burn in Poland as well — perhaps because that was precisely the home his family had fled.

What of those now living in California, or in the suburbs of New York City? They have not simply become outsiders. Rather, to the extent that they are still concerned with the Lower East Side as a place of ethnic origin and perhaps occasional refreshment, they participate in a cultural tradition of nostalgia for the immigrant cradle dating back nearly to the turn of the century (Wasserman 1987). To the extent that the Lower East Side is a declining Orthodox neighborhood, it may serve as a comforting reassurance to those who have moved away that what they gave up was destined for oblivion anyway. In this way, some connection to the neighborhood may legitimize and perpetuate forgetting, whereas an encounter with the thriving Orthodox population centers elsewhere might threaten the complacency of a nostalgic Judaism. This perception is implied in the following story, told to me by one of the young rabbis on the Lower East Side with whom I study:

> I happened to go to one of the synagogues on a Thursday morning. Maybe fifteen old men were there, and that was it. These people had come in, probably from Long Island — they were obviously people who had a lot of money and weren't involved in *Yiddishkayt* [Jewishness] at all — to make a bar-mitzvah for their kid. The grandfather *davened* [prayed] there. The kid didn't do anything but get an *aliyah* [he was summoned to recite the blessings before and after part of the Torah reading]. He hadn't been prepared at all, so, you know, they wanted to make him a bar-mitzvah, where are they going to take him? To *Zayde*'s [Grandfather's] synagogue. And this kid didn't even know the *brokhe* [blessing]. I mean he's standing up there at the *bime* [lectern], his legs are shaking, and the *shames* [sexton] has to prompt him on each word. . . .
>
> So these people come to the East Side the one time when they want a little *Yiddishkayt*, and that's what they see. They don't know there are tens of thousands of Orthodox Jews in Flatbush, in Williamsburg, in Boro Park — that place is

teeming with kids; they think this is it, this is the last remnant of *Yiddishkayt* in America.

Whether on the Lower East Side, in Brooklyn, in the suburbs, or elsewhere, forgetting—of text, folklore, meaning-invested geography—is a central fact of Jewish life in our times. The loss of a particular space, of a face-to-face everyday "community" of those sharing a common culture, is perhaps the smallest of three concentric registers of collective loss. A second is the loss of "tradition," of a set of lifeways passed along according to the model suggested by Tocqueville. The third is genocide, the destruction of an imagined national collective, the loss of a "people." Much as these forms of loss, especially the last, appear sacrosanct, I intend to emphasize here, by placing them within quotation marks, that they are indeed constructions—and losing them is a construction as well.

It is necessary that these constructions be made visible, not in order to debunk them (they are as real as anything, including our lives), but because they participate in forgetting and memory simultaneously, and we need to know which of these two masters we serve when we participate in construction. Memory is much more demanding, and may perhaps be served only at the cost of diminished ambitions. The efforts of ethnographers, folklorists, poets, and the like to counter collective forgetting—even when such efforts are archived or disseminated in various ways—do little to change the conditions blocking face-to-face intergenerational transmission of memory. Such efforts are essentially outside the community and in this sense hermetic, yet valid insofar as they satisfy the anamnestic urge of the producer.

A large color photographic print hangs in my living room. It depicts a sink, a radiator, a dirty towel, a cracked wall, a bench, and several Hebrew names engraved on a memorial stone plaque. Its richness of detail and depth of light are extraordinary. The beauty contained in the photograph stands not only against the vast unlikelihood that the synagogue it portrays will ever be restored to its former beauty, not only against the unlikelihood that anyone looking at the wall will see what is created by (not captured in) the photograph, but also against any likelihood that the synagogue would ever be lit adequately to display the photograph properly. The photograph rescues and takes, but does not return to its source.

And yet, my friend the photographer and "documenters" like him are also potential participants, capable of evoking momentary gaps in the otherwise prevalent miasma of oblivion. He came to the synagogue with me on a Sabbath morning, and I introduced him to the president of the congregation. The president pointed to the area above the Ark where the Torah scrolls are kept: "Now there's nothing here to photograph. This woodwork is all hand carved. On top—where you see that piece of red velvet, or whatever it is—there used to be carved wooden filigree, and in the middle of it the wood was carved in the shape of the priests' hands, with their fingers spread out. On top of that, above the lights on that little board there, was a carving of the Ten Commandments, with a gold crown, and on top of that was an eagle with its wings spread out."

I hadn't heard all this before. Some of the wood carvings have left their trace in darker patches of the velvet backing, but I would never have guessed at the proud eagle on top. Now the president and the photographer have shared it, and you know it as well, and we are seduced by memory once again.

Two

Europe's Indian, America's Jew
Modiano and Vizenor

For Greg Sarris and Menachem Prywes

The title of this chapter could easily be taken to imply a playful inversion of a straightforward analogy. I once thought of using that analogy as my title, writing it as a question in logic: "Europe : Jew :: America : Indian?" The question mark is not coy. Are the relations really that closely comparable—between two empires, on one hand, and two peoples within those empires, both repressed to the point of genocide, on the other hand—that they could be reduced to such a neat, schematic rendering? To do so would cancel out (as we used to say in math class) the specifics of each term in both matched pairs on either side of the double colon. I will not be offering a direct answer to one question implied by the title, which can be articulated thus: To what extent have Jews fulfilled the same function for the imagination of Europe as Indians have in the invention of America? The juxaposition that constitutes my title, then, is not at all meant to *equate* Europe with America, Indians with Jews. We will not gain any more insight by squeezing disparate yet comparable responses to disparate yet comparable situations into a simplistic prefabricated schema of domination and resistance.

I approach the four terms in my title indirectly, along three major lines of argument. The first is a feature of nation and empire building that Europe does share with America: the tendency to monumental representations. The second is the tendency each exhibits, but at dif-

9

ferent times and under very different pressures and circumstances, to create fascinated images of and to eulogize the other's victim. One effect of this displaced eulogization is to encourage amnesia about domination closer to home. Third, and most important, I will juxtapose "native" voices inside the respective empires as a way of resisting such amnesia and displacement.

Our tendency to think of relations as analogies—a Greek legacy, of course—is so powerful that I must list some fundamental ways in which this particular "analogy" is contaminated by any number of discrepancies. The American empire is to a large degree an extension of Europe, and so America's Indians are also to a large degree Europe's Indians. The peculiarities of American history are such that American identity is not nearly so thoroughly grounded in the tension between Christian triumphalism and Jewish survival as is European identity. Unlike Native Americans, Jews exist and express themselves as Jewish subjects in both Europe and America. Whereas the latter stages of Indian genocide were accomplished by "Americans" who identified with a relatively unified and monolingual culture, the Europe that Jews have survived in remained murderously fractious and culturally divided at least until the middle of this century. Unlike Native Americans in the United States, many Jews had acquired a relatively central position in European society before the Jewish genocide, which was both much more concentrated and single-minded and also more recent than that suffered by the pre-Columbian residents of the Americas.

These discrepancies should be borne in mind throughout this chapter, as I contrast fictions by Patrick Modiano and Gerald Vizenor. It is not enough to say that both are the voices of survivors, written after genocide, on the soil of genocide. Some of the difference between Modiano's cosmic cynicism and Vizenor's fantasy redemption may have to do with when the two books were written. When Modiano published his book in 1968, French Jewry might well have seemed doomed to a literary existence at best. Vizenor's, on the other hand, was published in 1988, in the midst of a Native American renewal that has seen a threefold increase in the number of self-identified Native Americans in recent decades.

Above all, Modiano's and Vizenor's brilliant voices successfully resist any effort to treat them as representatives of self-contained "cultures," to turn them into grist for the homogenizing mill of liberal anthropology. For anthropology, too, has its topoi: cultures and cultural motifs that serve as standard points of reference, enabling those in the "field" to recognize and recruit each other. Working beyond the common places of ethnography challenges disciplinary power and constitutes a bid for new powers. Thus Michael Herzfeld employs a classic rhetorical gesture to authorize his critical ethnography of the dialectic of modern Greek and European identities:

> Greece may be unique in the degree to which the country as a whole has been forced to play the contrasted roles of *Ur-Europa* and humiliated oriental vassal at the same time. These two roles might seem mutually incompatible, were it not for the fact that both imply inferiority to the "true" European of today. (1987: 19-20)

With one keystroke Herzfeld makes a double move, both mocking and mirroring the double move of European romantic nationalism that he is analyzing in these sentences. He points out—and demonstrates painstakingly throughout his text—the double bind of people cast as degenerate descendants of the glorious common ancestors they share with those who now enjoy the power to define them as Other. At the same time he makes an implicit argument that, because they have suffered the implication of inferiority, modern Greeks deserve the sympathetic ethnographic attention that he devotes to them. He grounds his writing not directly within the subordination of modern Greeks, but in counterpoint to the dichotomizing European discourse that he criticizes. His critical ethnography is written not only in the margins of Europe (as his subtitle proclaims), but in the margins of the text called Europe as well. Though Herzfeld's book is nothing if not sober, scholarly, and expensive, still he appears as a kind of anthropological trickster, undermining the certainties of European identity from what the production of that identity calls "within."

In this respect at least, contemporary Jews and Native Americans are in the same situation as contemporary Greeks. They are simultaneously seen as noble cultural ancestors of the groups that dominate them (Christian Europeans and white Americans, respectively) and denigrated as marginal and backward relics. For Native Americans, one symptom of this peculiar addition of insult to injury is that they are present in American consciousness more as totems of commodities

(Pontiac cars) and geographic boundaries of power (Manhattan, Massachusetts) than as "our" contemporaries. For Jews, the irony of this double attitude in its most seemingly benevolent form was expressed when the Bishop of Rome, in an unprecedented visit to the synagogue there, embraced the rabbi and referred to the Jews as "our older brothers." I found this rather moving, but on reflection—being a younger brother myself and having read the Jewish Bible—I was reminded of the power of sibling rivalry.

Fortunately, neither European Jews nor Native Americans rely solely on ethnographers to carry out the task of exposing the power illogic within which they are repeatedly placed. Nor do they always fall into the trap of performing a meliorative reinforcement of this illogic by presuming "finally" to offer a picture of what "their people" are really like,[1] a function that the best of humanistic ethnography seems ideally suited to perform.[2]

Modiano's *La Place de l'étoile* and Vizenor's *The Trickster of Liberty* avoid that ethnographic trap. In their own ways, both take care not to permit themselves to be taken as pure representatives of Indians or Jews. Vizenor insists, both in his own biography within the book and in the descriptions of his characters, on the uncompromised validity of "mixedblood" Indian identity. Indeed, the mixed heritage is drawn on as a resource in his and his characters' creative efforts to change without losing themselves. Whereas Modiano stays much more outside of his text, his hero, Schlemilovitch, has visions of revenge or redemption through entry into French literature, and thus might almost be taken as a double of his author. Yet Schlemilovitch, as we will see, tries desperately to "become French," but always with a cynical awareness of history that defeats his efforts either to root himself in "la France profonde" or to escape by becoming a normative Israeli. Modiano knows his hero's efforts are doomed from the start and thus marks his authorial distance. What both Vizenor and Modiano do, rather than fit in or declare an illusory solidarity of the oppressed, is instead to try cutting straight through the double bind of domination. Both of these short, picaresque, comic novels question the spatial symbolism of domination. Both authors proclaim that goal in their very titles. I hope to accomplish three things in these pages: first, to suggest the parallels and contrasts between Modiano's and Vizenor's respective scenes of writing; second, to show some of the contrasting techniques they use to achieve similar rhetorical goals; and third, to develop a bit their implicit critique of monuments.

Modiano's title refers simultaneously to the location of France's glory, the Arc de Triomphe, and to the topos of France's shame, the breast of the Jew on which the yellow star was worn. We know this from the cover of his book. The front shows a young man in a respectable raincoat, with a yellow star bearing the word *Juif* in place of the head, thus warning us in advance that this book will not repeat the pathetic attempt to establish the real person behind the stereotype. The back tells the story from which the title is drawn:

> In the month of June 1942, a German officer approaches a
> young man and says to him:
> "Pardon, monsieur, where is the Place de l'Etoile?"
> The young man indicates the left side of his chest.

There is no mystery about Modiano's title, then, and he doesn't even claim credit for it (although on the cover the yellow star is displaced from the chest to the head). The same few sentences are reprinted inside, at the beginning of the book, and there identified as "histoire juive." The attribution ironically inscribes Modiano's book within . . . not a Jewish "folklore" tradition, but a Jewish "history," which is inseparable from "story," tricksterlike, necessarily self-inventing and self-deconstructing as the condition of its own existence. This is a revealing contrast to the Arc de Triomphe, which anchors the tourist guide's Place de l'Etoile—"a sort of altar of French patriotism" that "remains as a majestic witness to our national destiny" (*Dictionnaire* 1964: 198). Such a stone edifice (placed, in a sense, at the center of the world, a sun with boulevards radiating outward) works to hold together the weakening link among French nationalism, progress, Revolution, and Empire. It also guards the phantasm of a unitary and unstoppable national destiny. Fortunately France also has room for voices like Modiano's, which question that phantasm and that link.

Vizenor's title refers to a scale model of the Statue of Liberty renamed and removed to a reservation in Minnesota. The cover of *his* book, rather than commenting on the title, seems more abstractly designed to inscribe the text within the University of Minnesota Press series on "emergent literatures" within which it has found a home. This rubric is puzzling. "Emergent literatures" certainly seems to fall into the same category as cultural "diversification"—a principle clearly consistent with a wide range of liberatory discourses. Yet the need to find ways to market such works creates a situation where their critical sting can too easily be made painless by creating a new category, a sort of *cordon sanitaire*, within which they can all be managed. There are several questions to be asked when works as different as *The Trickster of Liberty* and Clarice Lispector's Brazilian *écriture féminine* fall under the same rubric: "What are they emerging into? Are they merely being made available, archived, or do they *change* that into which they emerge? Can they emerge without abandoning that from which they emerge?" (see Godzich 1988).

Underscoring the subversive effect of the phrase "the trickster of liberty" by placing it against the obvious pun indicated by Modiano's cover helps guard against such sanitary management. Unlike the Place de l'Etoile, which existed before Modiano wrote his book, the Trickster of Liberty is erected only toward the end of Vizenor's book and finds its historical correlative only in 1989, after the book was published—about which more later. But while Vizenor's book was in press, the Statue of Liberty itself was the focus of a massive campaign of material and ideological rehabilitation. Vizenor's erasure of the statue and substitution of a trickster performs the same service as Modiano's story about the "other" star. It helps to dislodge the unquestioned, monumental place the edifice has occupied in our imaginations. To imagine Liberty as tricksterlike helps free us from the trance of our "national destiny" and awaken us to all the chances that dance around us in the present and in the past.

Both Modiano's and Vizenor's disruptions of the monumental metonymies of empire should be read as effective threats to the laborious work of instilling monumental respect. That the inculcation of monumental respect is indeed the project of disciplined work rather than magic is documented in a National Park Service directive regarding the St. Louis Gateway Arch:

> "Because the Gateway Arch is a National Memorial equal in dignity and grandeur to other great memorials and is becoming a symbol of St. Louis, it should be utilized in advertising, displays, cartoons, etc., with restraint." In making use of the arch, one should ask, "Is the proposed use

frivolous or ostentatious? . . . Is the Gateway Arch displayed
in its proportionate scale to other structures?" (quoted in Tuan
1974: 200)[3]

I suppose the mixedblood Chippewa Gerald Vizenor, looking at the
Gateway Arch, wouldn't have to be reminded of Walter Benjamin's
thesis that "there is no document of civilization which is not at the
same time a document of barbarism" (1969b: 256). Dissenting middle-
class intellectuals, on the other hand, usually treat artifacts like the
Gateway Arch as nothing more than banal efforts at boosterism, symbols of the overriding American drive for money. Modiano's revelation of the dark side of the "star," however, helps us to see that in
America, too, the monuments at the gateways of empire shut some
out and others in. The Gateway Arch and the Statue of Liberty, as
symbols of redemption, are for the primary use of those descended
from European immigrants, those who entered through the Golden
Door of the Golden Land. I imagine Miss Liberty is less thrilling to
those whose ancestors came in chains, or through Pacific ports, or up
from south of the border . . . or to those whose ancestors were here
long before Columbus came.

The Statue of Liberty, then, stands for the levelizing inclusion of a
certain set of internally differentiated immigrations. Native Americans are especially shut out because they are not included among the
immigrants and because (as the Gateway Arch makes clearer) they are
an embarrassing reminder that liberty will have its victims. The Arc
de Triomphe, of course, makes the latter point much more clearly: it is
a symbol of the carnivorous conquest of various nations in the name of
liberté, egalité, fraternité. The Napoleonic link between the French Empire and the Republican doctrine enunciated in the Declaration of the
Rights of Man that "sovereignty resides essentially in the nation" may
seem ironic (Der Derian 1989: 3), but it is hardly the first time in
"Western" history that people have been violently set free, whether
they liked it or not.[4]

Related to the meliorative "realism" I referred to earlier is the tendency, in the respective imperial contexts of America and Europe, to
valorize the other empire's vanquished Other. Within Europe, the
point is best made by shifting the focus a bit from the Place de l'Etoile
to the focus of anti-Jewish genocide — to Germany, where, long before

World War II, the exalted image of the Indian took hold as nowhere else in Europe:

> The German reader single[d] out the Indian as the one exotic race with which he was and still seems ready to sympathize, and even to identify himself. That the Germans should have this special relationship, stronger than that of the French or English, is traceable, most likely, to the fact that Germany was a late comer to colonialism, and never encountered the Indian as opposing colonization; that her contact with the Red Man was "only literature." (Vagts 1957: 17)

The reader may supply her own critical reflections on the engendering of the German reader as male, of Germany as female, and of Native Americans as the Red Man. I want to insist a bit on the suggestion that, unlike direct colonial encounters where the colonizer's image of the native initially veers between noble and ignoble savagery and eventually coalesces into a stereotype of irredeemable barbarism (Pearce 1988), an empire that has no direct conflict with a certain set of "natives" can continue to draw on that group as a cultural model or as an exemplary victim of someone else's excesses.

In the German case, the most spectacular example of this is Karl May, who began publishing his novels about the American West in 1892 and is still a bestselling author a century later.[5] May's most successful novel is named after its Indian hero, *Winnetou*. In a preface to the first volume of that novel, May mourns the unjust passing of the Indian:

> Many questions arise, and this one in particular: What could this race have achieved, had it been given the opportunity? What characteristic cultural forms will forever be lost to mankind with the annihilation of this people? The dying Indian could not be integrated into the white world, because of his unique character. Was that reason enough to kill him? Could he not have been saved?
> But what use are such questions in the face of certain death? What good are reproaches where help is no longer possible? I can only lament, but change nothing; only grieve, but not bring a single dead back to life. (1979: xiv)

Presumably the words are intended not so much as those of May, but

rather as those of his impossibly idealized German pioneer hero, Old
Shatterhand; the distinction is not important. That both author and
hero were wrong about the fate of the Indians is cause for hope, but
not the main point here. Apparently his esthetic *required* that the noble
Red Man be doomed. In a critical essay, Peter Uwe Hohendahl suggests why this may be so. May's anticapitalism is expressed in his negative portrayals of "Yankee traders" (Hohendahl 1989: 219). His
vision of human solidarity is expressed on one hand by the ideal group
discipline and precise unity of his favorite tribe, the Apaches, and on
the other by the depiction of fraternal relations between true pioneer
"men of the West"—honest, self-reliant, and tough—and individual
Indian men bearing the same qualities. Hence May dreamed of a new
order of human solidarity against individual greed and the profit motive (230-31). But if this vision were to come about through bloodless
revolution, as May insisted, it could perhaps only be sustained by an
appeal to the inevitability of progress. And progress means the Indian,
with all his potential virtues, must pass on for the sake of greater human good. Once again the compatibility of the elegiac mode with the
smooth history of genocide is reconfirmed.

A slightly different facet of the notion of the Red Man—here not so
much his virility as his mobility, something that the writer can only
express as unabashed fantasy longing—is contained in Kafka's fragment called "The Wish to Be a Red Indian":

> If one were only an Indian, instantly alert, and on a racing
> horse, leaning against the wind, kept on quivering jerkily over
> the quivering ground, until one shed one's spurs, for there
> needed no spurs, threw away the reins, for there needed no
> reins, and hardly saw that the land before one was smoothly
> shorn heath when horse's head and neck would be already
> gone. (1979: 242)

On one hand Kafka seems here to enlist himself as a participant in the
German romanticization of the Indian. In contrast, say, to the infinite
sorrow of "The Bucket Rider," where the narrator denied coal is carried off "into the regions of the ice mountains and . . . lost for ever"
(Kafka 1970: 187), there seems at first nothing original about the image of the Indian. Its pathos is inseparable from its banality. But at a
closer look we see that there is in fact no image of "the Indian" con-

tained here, except for that which the history of the word itself evokes. And there is no static entity here, but rather an experience of free motion. The reader is placed on that racing horse, and there is no room for stereotype, only sensation.

At least one more level is discernible within this *mise-en-abîme* of othering, brought forward into the present: the German admiration and concern for the bitter fate of the "Red Man" is available, post-Holocaust, as a target of contemporary American sarcasm. Thus, in the course of a travelogue of the Great Plains, Ian Frazier quotes without comment a remark by a young German hitchhiker, who explains that he is a graduate student in anthropology:

> He looked at the landscape and said, "Ach! Zo vlat. . . . Za vite people haff destroyed zo many uff za Indians' sacred places."
> I looked at him. "What is your name?" I asked.
> "Gerhard Stadler," he said.
> I asked him to spell it. He did, and then shut up. (Frazier 1989: 36)

Frazier represents himself putting the presumptuous young German in his place. The "eye dialect" reserved for the foreigner and the taking down of his name properly spelled are acts of journalistic policing, doubtless enough to convey to an American reader the smug suggestion that any German is hardly in a position to talk about genocide.[6]

But if this linguistic suggestion by Frazier isn't enough to reinforce the comforting illusion that the historical burden of genocide is someone else's problem, we can rely on yet another monument—the U.S. Holocaust Museum currently being erected in Washington, D.C. A liberal interpretation of the motives for establishing this institution would be that the museum will stand as a moral lesson about intolerance. I suspect it will function more effectively as a bastion of the message that America saved the Jews and is saving Israel now. More important—since remembering the Holocaust is hardly a central project to all American Jews, let alone the majority of U.S. citizens—by advertising that America has the space in its heart and in its capital to commemorate genocide committed elsewhere, the genocidal origins of the United States will be further occluded. How, then, could or should Native Americans react to the fact that there is a U.S.

Holocaust Museum but no U.S. Memorial to the Slaughtered Native Americans—especially if they want to avoid offending Jews in the process of expressing any opinion whatsoever?

The strategic response is certainly neither to become caught up in a competition for priority in recognition of genocide nor to assert the sameness of all empires and all genocides. There might be more to be learned through a careful tracing, along back paths not already guarded by the intellectual patrols of neoimperialism, of the border lines where comparative experiences of imperial victimization and resistance meet and separate.[7] These paths and borders, of course, are not to be found on any Cartesian plane, nor will they stay in the same place as we change our relation to them. As a provisional critical starting point from the Jewish "side," I might indicate that, so long as Jews were useful to Christian Europe as an object lesson in the degradation of the unredeemed soul, some level of Jewish existence was tolerated even when Jews were murdered wholesale; but when the legitimating notion of universal individual redemption gave way to the territorial, this-earthly dream of collective progress through the defined nation-state, there was eventually no room for the Jews at all. On the Native American side, it should be possible to discern the beginnings of a critical trajectory from three linked points: first, the connection in North American settler ideology between collective expansion and individual sedentarism (cf. Carter 1988, especially chapter 5); second, the presumption that all Indians were alike, and thus could be indefinitely shifted further toward the "underused" west without harm to them selves or each other; and third, the idea that the only hope for Native Americans to survive was as individual Christians (Berkhofer 1979: 138, 152, 151).

Meanwhile, reading can help us to locate, beyond the shadow cast by these monuments, spaces for European Jewish life after World War II or for Native American life on the North American continent. It would seem that the primary space for European Jews today is within the book[8]; Native Americans have, as well, their poor and struggling reservations. Modiano's text, in any case, resolutely refuses allegiance to any place outside the book, and, as I will describe, his antihero is punished for his one slip, his one attempt to claim such an exterior allegiance. Vizenor's numerous protagonists hang onto their "wild baronage," but neither their identities nor their collective exploits are contained within it.

Caveat Lector: First Variation

My comparison of *The Trickster of Liberty* and *La Place de l'étoile* is grounded neither in oeuvre nor in author's biography. Both Modiano and Vizenor have published several books,[9] but I am writing about two fictions that came to me relatively accidentally. Although I can hardly pretend to erase all traces of an "ethnic writing" effect from my own rhetoric, it is not the enabling situation of the two authors that primarily concerns me but, as David Lloyd puts it, "those processes of [their] writing which sustain a minorness resistant to the proprieties of representation" (1987: 175). Far be it from me to explain, to pin down, to fix. For as Lloyd also makes clear, deterritorialization—a refusal to lock identity in place—is critical to this minorness. Thus Modiano's protagonist derides the French fetishism of the soil of native regions. Vizenor's oralizing, landscapizing tricksters explicitly signal the ambiguity of location, as when one of them, homeless, declares his allegiance to a portable fatherland whose creation is attributed to a Jewish name: "Sylvan Goldman invented the nest [shopping] cart, and I declared the tandem a sovereign state on low wheels" (67).

Caveat Lector: Second Variation

La Place de l'étoile is not long, but it contains such a variety of literary and historical references that I cannot possibly know all of them. I don't even know in some cases whether a reference is historical or literary; sometimes I'm not sure whether the reference is borrowed or appears for the first time in Modiano's book. We American readers in general might wish for a skeleton key to *La Place de L'étoile*, because we are not so well acquainted with the history of European venality. My claim in any case is that virtually all of these names are dropped, poured on, farcically; we need not value them the way the antihero Schlemilovitch does in order to catch the savage humor in their deployment.

Anyway, a skeleton key might prove to be more than a macabre metaphor. Anthropologists have traded real skeletons for so long, creating such resentment in the process, that Vizenor comes to fantasize the remains of anthropologists as a sideshow at an international tribal exposition (98).[10] The native's skeleton, so dear to physical anthropologists, is also a perfect trope for the anthropological fetish of a bloodless, fleshless "social structure." Elsewhere Vizenor has helped to explain this fetish by writing of liberal social science as a variation on tragedy, which seals off in silence and isolation the comic voice of the trickster (1989). A similar tendency, criticized by the great historian Salo Baron as "the lachrymose conception in Jewish history" (1964), long prevailed in Jewish secular scholarship. That Jewish secular scholarship—originating in Germany as *Wissenschaft des Judentums*— openly saw traditional Jewish communal life as doomed, and set itself the goal of providing Judaism with a decent burial. Fortunately, neither anthropology nor *Wissenschaft des Judentums* was quite right: there are still walking, talking Jews and Indians.[11]

The Other, dead or alive, is an almost inexhaustible symbolic resource. Jews and Indians are invented by those who Other them as good or bad according to the needs of circumstances (Berkhofer 1979: 28, 110–11; Pearce 1988; Gilman 1985: introduction). Under some circumstances, where the dilemmas of the dominant, collectively imagined self do not call forth genocidal responses, this interaction offers the minority group a space to survive through the symbolic and material goods it provides. Thus Vizenor discusses complex negotiations for the export of "wild" ginseng from the White Earth reservation in Minnesota to East Asia, where it is highly valued. Thus Jews survived in Central and Eastern Europe for centuries as a middleman minority, plying alcohol concessions, trading in textiles, and sometimes making up out of whole cloth news of the wide world when it was demanded of them (Kugelmass 1980; D. Kahan, cited in Kugelmass and Boyarin 1983: 15).[12]

How do I avoid at least a blind fall into the trap of that exploitative fallacy? The mere assertion of my Jewishness, far from enabling me to leap over the trap, would more likely propel me into it. It may be that a degree of autocannibalism (self-absorption?) is inevitable for an academic writing about the problematics of "his own" collective identity. Let the reader (who, of course, tomorrow will be me) beware—and revise wherever necessary and possible.

Caveat Lector: Third Variation

I have an ulterior motive. In some measure at least, my engagement of an elite Native American text in this essay is intended to help prepare me for my work in and about Israel and Palestine. I participate in America, though I rarely think of myself as an American. I am implicated in the history of Israel, though I am hardly an Israeli. I want to acknowledge some of the ways in which as an American (an identity I usually explicitly deny) I benefit from a prior obliteration of the Native American Other. This tangential engagement of a legacy of domination in which I share might help prevent me from following the common tendency to identify some originary source of oppression (Zionism, patriarchy, Christianity, European imperial nationalism), from which I could safely dissociate myself.[13]

But given this explicitly historicizing and political project, I must stress that I am not writing of "the Indians" or of "the Jews." I am referring rather to the stereotyped currency of identity. The stereotypes have an interesting and contingent life of their own. Thus, for example, both authors play with the idea of Jews and Indians as in some way regarded as Orientals. Vizenor, without announcing himself, retraces the hypothesized original trek across the frozen Bering Strait when several of his tricksters make their careers in China. And Modiano's Schlemilovitch, in his misogynist adventure as a white slaver, balks at the prospect of kidnapping a young French noblewoman for sale to an Arab noble: "Transform Eleanor of Aquitaine into an inmate of a bordello! The idea revolted him. One can bear the name Schlemilovitch and still have a bit of compunction at the bottom of one's heart. . . . He would never deliver this princess, this fairy, this saint to the Saracens" (126–27). Here Modiano presents us the Jew as Crusader. Even with a Jewish name, Schlemilovitch declares, one can remain civilized enough to side with Christian Europe against the Orient.

It's almost time to have done with my own critical compunctions, but before I do, let me discuss the scenes of torture in both books. Schlemilovitch's tormentors are Nazis and agents of the Israeli secret service (by the end of *Place de l'étoile*, there is no distinction between the two). In *Liberty*, the torturers are animal researchers, but the two dogs White Lies and Chickenlips have by that point in the book become such animated tricksters that the reader joins in anger at "those assholes in life sciences." And hasn't much of anthropology long aspired to be one of the "life sciences?"

Vizenor will do anything to get anthropologists to stop being so damned serious; he even has one of the dogs "hobble[] into the library . . . and mount[] the anthropologist at the kitchen table" (xii). Modiano, too, comments on anthropology, when his hero travels to a pristine Alpine village in Haute-Savoie to kidnap a woman for white slavery: "Above all, avoid arousing their suspicion. Stifle my ethnological curiosity, like Lévi-Strauss. The Savoyards are more clever than the Indians of Parana. Don't look at their daughters like a pimp would, or they'll guess my Oriental ancestry" (100). The clutch of associations here is consistent with Schlemilovitch's fanatic embrace of anti-Semitic stereotypes. Lévi-Strauss's Jewishness is revealed (and his "stifling" pretense of ahistorical, structural objectivism lampooned), while the "white" Europeans are simultaneously exoticized and exposed as potential victims of Semitic ethnopimping.

But training, if not blood, will out, and at some point I, too, start thinking like an anthropologist, wondering whether the contrast between Modiano's comic rage and Vizenor's comic tease (whose mascot is White Lies, the dog that reappears in every doggie generation) is connected solely to the relative pace and intensity of the two genocides, or whether there are "cultural" reasons involved as well. Are there Jewish sources of Modiano's energy, Native American sources for Vizenor's playfulness?

Jewish messianism is obviously out of the question for Modiano. There's no hope of redemption at *La Place de l'étoile*; there are only the ruins of the hopes of the past. Modiano's antilogic is inscribed within a "space of death" (Taussig 1984). This space of death would seem to have no room for the trickster; Schlemilovitch is closer to a pantheon of pariahs, like "Franz Kafka, the older brother of Charlie Chaplin" (42).[14] The pariah, as outsider and arriviste, effectively disrupts the fetishism of territory, as when Schlemilovitch reveals that imitation is the sincerest form of mockery:

> I only knew the French provinces through the mediation of the Michelin guide, and of certain authors such as François Mauriac. One text by this native of the Landes moved me

especially: *Bordeaux, or Adolescence.* I recall Mauriac's surprise
when I passionately recited to him his beautiful prose: "The
city where we were born, where we were a child, an
adolescent, is the only one we are forbidden to judge. She is
part of us, she is ourselves, we bear her in ourselves. The
history of Bordeaux is the history of my body and my soul."
(56-57)

But Modiano refuses (or is not yet ready) to counterpose to this territorial fetishism a "Jewish" insistence on the possibilities of fulfillment
in time. In fact, the only temporal power granted to Schlemilovitch
and to his employer/accomplice, Charles Lévy-Vendôme, is a negative
disruption of "pagan," cyclical time. The latter, Orientalized in a red
turban, declares "they need me at Constantinople to perform the
gradual cessation of the cycle. The seasons will change bit by bit, first
spring, then summer." (143). No, decidedly, Schlemilovitch is not in
the business of recuperating the ancient resources of Jewish tradition
to help mend the world. In *Place de l'étoile* the only effect a Jew can
have on the course of time is by assuming the position of the Oriental
and thereby slowing time down.

   For Vizenor, on the other hand, Trickster remains as a genuine
source not only of unpredictability but also of renewal. Vizenor's
tricksters are able to "relume" (Vizenor's word) and upset the flow of
domination in both time and space. One of his tricksters "carried a
holster to shoot time, dead time on the clock" (40). But this desire to
stop the tyrannical rule of clock time is hardly a feature of Native
American culture as opposed to Jewish culture. Perhaps it is something that both share with revolutionary culture, as documented by
Walter Benjamin's quotation of a French revolutionary poem about
"new Joshuas" shooting at the clock towers (1969b: 262).

   With regard to space, Vizenor both documents and undermines the
territorial fixing of a subaltern people. His "mixedblood" Chippewas
seize the opportunity to retain a scrap of land and declare themselves
"tribal heirs to a wild baronage." The whites see it as poor land; that's
why they leave it to the natives. In the utilitarian valuation of the settler Americans, the idea of a wild baronage appears oxymoronic, as
Tocqueville wrote: "The wonders of inanimate nature leave [Ameri-
cans] cold. . . . This magnificent vision. . . . is always flitting before

[their] mind[s]" (cited in Mitchell 1987: 1). But these native "barons" are not duped: they know better than to turn White Lies and Chickenlips into their serfs.

There are anti–Cartesian chronotopic conflations in both books, but here again Modiano leans toward comic despair, Vizenor toward a mocking fantasy redemption. Toward the end of *La Place de l'étoile*, Schlemilovitch decides to set sail for Israel. In a conversation with the Israeli Admiral Levy, in which the latter expresses his admiration for the liberal traditions of France and the sweetness of its countryside, Schlemilovitch reaches — just this one time — for a positive identity, an identification with the Israeli authority figure: "I'm not altogether French, admiral, I'm a French JEW. French JEW" (178). Schlemilovitch is immediately arrested on an implicit charge of diasporic degeneracy and thrown into the hold. When he is taken out, he finds himself in the Paris of the Nazi Occupation, where the rest (almost) of the action will take place. This fade without transition from the sea near Israel to occupied Paris belies the general assumption that the Occupation is in the past, that the establishment of Israel has put all that behind us. The return to that seeming past is the nightmare complement of Benjamin's revolutionary suspension of temporality. There has in fact been neither revolution nor liberal progress. The last sections of this book, which was published in 1968, might be taken as a cri de coeur against the very resumption of bourgeois society after the disaster of World War II.

Vizenor's most striking bending of time, place, and genre boundaries pictures Tune Brown, one of his tricksters, getting an honorary degree at Berkeley, in the notable presence of the famous ethnographer Alfred L. Kroeber. The scene is reminiscent of Woody Allen's Zelig. But there is no Zelig here; when Vizenor's tricksters change guise, they don't experience Zelig's vertigo. The absence of that anxiety leaves room for Vizenor to perform an anamnestic recovery of Ishi, last member of a California Indian tribe, famous in the history of anthropology for being put on museum display as a living relic. Vizenor mixes the three genres of historiographic reconstruction, scholarly citation, and invented oration in a single sentence:

> "[Roy] Wagner [in *The Invention of Culture*] tells how Ishi, the
> last survivor of the Yahi tribe in California, 'brought the
> world into the museum,' where he lived and worked after our

capture," Tune confessed as he threw his shirt and the ribbons
from his braids to the audience. (47)

It would be self-defeating to ask us to revisit Ishi as a tragic figure. The
only way Ishi[15] can be rescued is through a comic celebration, bringing dead anthropologists and Indians together with living scholars and
invented Indians onto the same page. Fortunately, the page is willing.

Schlemilovitch is more of an iconoclast than a trickster, even
though his method of breaking the idols is tricksterlike: he places himself inside them, and they burst because they cannot contain him. It
may be plausible to relate this to the irredeemable, rapacious misogyny of Schlemilovitch's iconoclasm. While in the first part of *La Place
de l'étoile* he aims to subvert the sanctity of French letters and patriotism, he subsequently abandons scholasticism for a concentrated as-
sault on the purity of French Catholic womanhood. Certainly Modiano
intends this as a characteristically transgressive assertion of the stereotype
of the Jew as white slaver—a stereotype that once again reared its ugly
head in the city of the Maid of Orleans just about the time *La Place de
l'étoile* was published (Morin 1971).[16] I imagine that for most readers,
when the book was first published these passages were taken as an attack
not on women, but on the institutions of the church and nobility. They
can no longer be given that charitable reading. I have no choice but to
recoil and renounce my affiliation with the author of *La Place de l'étoile* on
reading the passage where Schlemilovitch describes his "idyllic week"
with a debauched countess, who collaborates with his fantasies of raping
"the duchess of Berry . . . Bossuet, Saint Louis . . . Joan of Arc, the
count of Toulouse and General Boulanger" (135). Unlike the dominating
discourse of anti-Semitism, this sexual violence is never turned against
Schlemilovitch. The homosocial compact of literature (Sedgwick 1985),
even between "the (male) Jews" and their victimizers, remains intact.

The discourse of gender in Vizenor's text, written twenty years
later, seems indeed to indicate a measure of progress. His critico-
fictional prologue focuses on the androgyny of Trickster, who is embodied in a female trickster storyteller named Sergeant Alex. The
tragically fixated Euro-anal anthropologist Eastman Shicer insists on
pinning her down as a specimen: "*Alexina*, why did you disown your
given name? . . . Worried about being identified as a woman?" (xii).[17]
Another member of the Browne family of tricksters becomes a priest

named Father Mother. Vizenor also presents a mixedblood male professor with the ambiguous name of Terrocious Pan-Anna and empathetically describes trickster Tulip Browne's recoil from Pan-Anna's sexually predatory efforts to capture her via a presumed racial connection. On the other hand, Vizenor engages in a good bit of lesbian-feminist bashing of his own (80 ff.).

Beyond the gap in time and place between Modiano's writing and Vizenor's, the contrast in their use of gender leads toward the European psychoanalytic question of male ego formation. Vizenor's tricksters are multiple, although all members of the same clan; Modiano's text is ferociously monological, his narrator voraciously egotistical. Vizenor creates his resilient tricksters through the resources of a rich orality and kin ideology, which, if not intact, remain reinventable. Schlemilovitch, Zeliglike, obsessed with figures of the colonizing Other irredeemably inside him, can't even make up his mind on a literary model for his own death: "Nerval or Kafka? Suicide or the sanatorium?" (169).

But Schlemilovitch's musings are not in the nature of a serious philosophical reflection on the postgenocidal Jewish condition. Nor do his references have anything to do, except perhaps by way of yet another parody, with the idea that Jews are "people of the book." Insofar as it is grounded at all, the ground is intertextual, a bitter critique of Sartre's thesis that the Jew is a reflection of the non-Jewish gaze. The Jew portrayed in Modiano's book struggles through bitter satire with and against the one-dimensional existence he is granted by Sartre—whereas Vizenor's characters struggle with and against the richer, but still reified and stereotyped, way they are represented in ethnography. Through his critique, Schlemilovitch finds a point of reconciliation and solidarity with his father, presented as a gauche wholesaler from New York dressed in a mauve suit and Kentucky green shirt:

> I wanted a policeman to stop us. I would have explained it to the French once and for all: I would have repeated that for twenty years we'd been perverted by one of their own, an Alsatian. He had affirmed that the Jews would not exist if the *goys* didn't deign to pay attention to them. Thus we have to attract their attention by means of motley clothes. For us Jews, it's a question of life and death. (68)[18]

This moment of ironic solidarity is enabled by a contest of textualizations. Schlemilovitch endlessly complicates his young author's bid to gain admittance into the sphere of elite French literate culture by an original satire of that culture. Above and beyond all the disguises from French and Jewish literature and history that he adopts, Schlemilovitch is a negative image, a parodic extension and breathless summary of "Marcel"/Proust:[19] "I remember that Des Essarts compared our friendship to that which united Robert de Saint-Loup and the narrator of Remembrance of Things Past" (21). Thus La Place de l'étoile is also a retrospective evaluation, après Holocauste, of the assimilationist pretensions of the French "Israelites."

If Schlemilovitch remains more of a self-conscious cynic than a clownlike trickster, it is not because Jews are inexperienced at surviving by changing. It may be rather that in his author Modiano's view, culture is over; creative transformation is no longer possible, and the only hope for breathing space is in parody. Certainly we are given no clue that there are available internal Jewish resources that might serve such transformation. Indeed, Schlemilovitch/Modiano holds in abeyance the question whether there are "real Jews" existing outside of the reactive Sartrian dialectic. There is no midrashic textual heterodoxy in Schlemilovitch's narrative, unless it is reflected in the general tactic of guerrilla semantics, the forceful reappropriation of meaning for survival. In the decomposed European modernist tradition within which Modiano is still writing, heterodoxy can only take this relentlessly negative form.

Does this mean, in fact, that Trickster never lived or has died in Europe, that there is nothing at all of Trickster in the figure of Schlemilovitch? If the "hero"-victim dichotomy of European high culture is the proper antithesis of Trickster's ambiguity, this should not blind us to figures very much like Trickster in Jewish and other "Western" folklores—characters who survive by changing themselves as they point out and work through the frozen forms of their cultural surroundings. These stories are popular everywhere because they help living people negotiate the need for boundaries and the resistance to boundaries. We can grant these figures their due without denying the unique genius and central elaboration of the trickster motif in a range of Native American worlds.

Like the cynical pariah Schlemilovitch, then, Vizenor's tricksters are like him in that they also subvert their creator's authority, invading and deconstructing the university that constitutes Vizenor's base of operations. His prologue pays passing and ambivalent tribute to a contemporary pioneer of "Native American literature": "Momaday, of course, the most quoted and least read" (xiii).[20] Against what he identifies as Momaday's tragic view, however, Vizenor embraces impurity, as when Terrocious Pan-Anna explains that his father took the last name from the Pan-American Exposition of 1901, in which the father had been an exhibit. Vizenor insists that the real Indians are the mixedbloods (118). Transgressing his own renunciation of the anthropological tragic mode, he enlists the support of the authorization of traditional orality in the criticism of dissident folklorists such as Dell Hymes and Dennis Tedlock, at the same time contentiously authorizing his own *book*: "If you don't believe what tribal people say in my stories, then I don't believe what whites have said in those stories printed in your law books" (145–46).

Both books seem to end arbitrarily; neither has a teleological plot. In his "last" chronotopic shift, Schlemilovitch finds himself on Sigmund Freud's couch but resolutely refuses psychoanalysis. For Schlemilovitch, history is a nightmare from which there is no hope of awakening, because he is relentlessly *in* it, always being spatially confined, fatally and literally so when he attempts a sentimental voyage to the land of his ancestors (188).[21] For Vizenor's tricksters, there is no fundamental, unchanging nightmare. Not only do they retain a problematic sovereignty over their wild baronage, at the end their solution to material survival is to become, in a sense, Jews, active in tricksterlike hustling commerce, like Schlemilovitch's father the kaleidoscope king.

For Schlemilovitch, America exists only insofar as his father is a failing businessman in New York. Is this because America is, here again, seen as a blank slate, which does not offer even the inverted potential for identity contained in *Anti-Semite and Jew?* Central to the idea of "America" is the assertion that history is not merely ineffectual but ideally absent altogether, that a direct correspondence between human society and natural law is possible in the New World (Jehlen 1986: 3). Indeed, the greater invisibility of genocide in America may be related to the general devaluation of history here compared to Europe.

Here we return to the problematics pointed to by Herzfeld with which I began: the incorporation of the Other as both mythic ancestor and allegory of degradation. Native Americans would seem to be even more problematic as "ancestors" for European Christian settlers than Jews for European Christian civilization. The relatively recent appellation "Native Americans" doubtless represents a liberal attempt at incorporating the Other. Yet the term masks one of the basic causes of the European settlers' genocide: the unbearable presence of human beings who contradicted the "virgin land" ideology of the American incarnation (Smith 1970). Thus the sculpture by Horatio Greenough titled *Rescue Group*, showing a giant, godlike European stopping a naked Indian clad in a phallic sort of loincloth from slaughtering a European woman and child, is aptly used as the frontispiece to Roy Harvey Pearce's *Savagism and Civilization*. First by being here, then by resisting encroachment, and finally by their failure to be readily assimilable, the Indians were inevitably trapped in the symbolically linked roles of threat to white womanhood and illegitimate dweller in the land. Like the Statue of Liberty, the Gateway Arch, and the U.S. Holocaust Museum, the ideology of the pure and virgin land had no place for "Native Americans."

Can a similar analysis be made concerning the Jews? Certainly the Jews were an awkward reminder that the very same people who were around during the life of Jesus had rejected his message. But they were also a persistent challenge, a reminder that the missionary task of Christianity had not yet been completed—and, insofar as their conversion was linked to the Second Coming, Jewish souls were prize game for Christian hunters. It would seem, as I suggested earlier, that only when this dominant rationale for the irritating fact of continued distinctive Jewish existence became inadequate did an essentializing suspicion of the Jews harden into the conviction that they constituted the fly in the ointment of European solidarity and progress.

The question of how "minorities" are exploited and excluded in the reproduction of domination is inseparable from the various conceptions they and the dominant group form of their integrability into the state. Both Modiano's and Vizenor's works are problematic as inscriptions of ethnicity in the legitimating culture of the dominant group.

Modiano, of course, writes in French, not a Jewish language. Vizenor writes in English, and the destabilizing potential of *The Trickster of Liberty* is tamed by the suggestion that it belongs in the affirmative action category of emergent literatures. I say this not to suggest that their dissident claims need to be demystified, and not only because even resistant literatures often have their origin in imperial narrative (see Adorno 1986: 8-9; González-Echevarria 1987: 128), but also because demystifying critiques often fail "to address some of the crucial ways in which myth and history achieve their emotional potency, for the critics of whatever kind adopt a mode of reasoning which is not that of the myths" (Kapferer 1988: 40).

Rather, I want to conclude by pointing to the elements in both books, growing out of the authors' choices to criticize society through pariah iconoclasm and tricksterism, which have proven ironically prophetic. At one point after his arrest by the Israelis, Schlemilovitch finds himself in a concentration camp for recalcitrant Diaspora Jews. There are indeed concentration camps in Israel now,[22] not for entire Jewish families and communities, but for thousands of Palestinian men who, like the Zionists once did, are struggling to secure a homeland for themselves and for their people in Diaspora. And Vizenor's story of a Chinese deal to build a Trickster of Liberty statue on the White Earth reservation has found its heroic, hence tragic, realization in the defiant symbolism and martyrdom of Tiananmen Square.[23] These connections suggest once again the relevance of reading and writing to the interrelated possibilities of Statues of Liberty and restriction to reservations, of concentration camps and Arcs de Triomphe. This chapter could hardly serve as an adequate response to that suggestion, but I hope at least to have underscored the urgency of our collaborating on a comparative study of Otherings in the consolidation of the dominant collective self.

Three

The Former Hôtel Moderne
Between Walter Benjamin and Polish Jews
in Paris

I. Markers

What used to be the Hôtel Moderne on the Place de la République in Paris is now a Holiday Inn. Once upon a time, mass leftist political meetings were held there. The place is still referred to as "the former Hôtel Moderne" when the Parisian Yiddish daily announces the meeting place for busloads of mourners headed for the Jewish section of the Parisian municipal cemetery at Bagneux. The phrase is especially poignant in connection with funerals, since it stands as a motto for the experience of an entire generation of Polish Jewish immigrants in Paris, suggesting the evanescence of the new European culture they dedicated themselves to while still in Eastern Europe, as well as its afterimage in memory.

II. Deferment

I spent the academic year of 1982–83 in Paris doing fieldwork toward a dissertation in anthropology on this immigrant group (see J. Boyarin 1991).[1] During that year as well, the Suhrkamp edition of the complete works of Walter Benjamin was completed with the two volumes of his *Passagen-Werk* (in English sometimes called the Arcades project)—or more precisely, the collected drafts and notes for his planned but uncompleted magnum opus on nineteenth-century Paris.

The focus of these fragments is the glass-roofed shopping arcades built in Paris during the nineteenth century, which Benjamin took as emblems of that epoque's dream of an end to class-based historical strife in a consumerist utopia. I had already found various texts by Benjamin of indispensable help in my earlier work on the fragmented memory of East European Jewish culture and eagerly assumed that the *Passagen-Werk* would help me to comprehend my own fieldwork in Paris. Perhaps for fear that my obsession with Benjamin would overshadow my collective portrait of the immigrants, I have waited to write about the connection between them until that ethnography was finished.

III. The Dream of Paris

The immigrants came to Paris already at one social remove from a traditional Jewish culture that rewarded piety and strictly controlled daily behavior. For most, the link to that traditional culture was interrupted by a proletarian childhood in one of Poland's manufacturing or commercial cities and participation in left Zionist, Bundist, or Communist youth organizations. Some fled for political reasons and some fled unemployment. But the image of Paris that for Benjamin was epitomized by the shopping arcades known as *Passages*—that of the ultimate city that has conquered the vagaries of history and nature in a completely rational, completely esthetic civilization—played its role in their decision to come to Paris as well. The staging of international exhibitions heightened both of these motivations. The exhibitions offered a chance for foreign nationals to enter France, while they simultaneously heightened the brilliance of Paris. One man told me that he had wanted to come to the Paris World's Fair in 1936 but his father forbade it, saying, "The stones of Paris are *treyf*" (not-kosher); instead, he arrived as a refugee in 1945.

Whenever they arrived, the bulk of the immigrants immediately began working in the clothing industry, manufacturing the images of the city Benjamin called "the city of mirrors" (1983: 1047). But those who arrived before World War II had only a few years either for the dream that enough backbreaking work would bring them personal peace and prosperity or for the dream that dogged organization of the workers would progressively redeem the entire world. The mass immigration of Jews from Eastern Europe in the interwar period was quickly followed by Nazi occupation and mass deportation.

IV. Bloodstains on a Map

The map of Paris has changed since the war. The annual commemoration of the Warsaw Ghetto uprising begins at a certain spot from which Jewish children were deported; the plaque there testifies to the mark of the event on the geography of Paris, and on the memory of the immigrants. Unlike the Paris Commune, which Benjamin describes in his *Theses on the Philosophy of History* as a messianic moment (for him, implying the fullness of memory), the occupation of Paris represents a moment when much of the past was lost irretrievably. Its shadow remains over the Parisian Jewish community today.[2]

V. The Place of Memory

Many of the arcades still exist. Benjamin encountered the arcades already faded and treated them as oracles from the past. Although they must have been surrounded by freshly arrived, active immigrants (not all of them East European Jews) in the 1930s, these workers seem to find no place in his notes. I, on the other hand, encountered the immigrants, faded themselves, while some of the arcades retain their place as homes for the textile industry.

Benjamin refers to the arcades as "Architectures in which we relive in dreams the lives of our parents and grandparents, as the embryo in its mother relives the life of the species" (1983: 1054). My own mother learned (perhaps in the same year that Benjamin wrote that phrase) that ontogeny recapitulates phylogeny. We no longer believe so, but we have learned—notably from Benjamin—that we reflect and contain our own history in unexpected ways. We also betray tradition if we assert historical continuities in an overly facile way.

Much has been made, in fact, of Benjamin's so-called Jewish messianism. This discussion is grounded in certain texts by Benjamin, especially his late "Theses on the Philosophy of History," and also on his lifelong friendship with Gershom Scholem. Those moments of memory that "flash up at a moment of danger" Benjamin called "the sign of a Messianic cessation of happening, or, put differently, a revolutionary chance in the fight for an oppressed past." He concluded the "Theses" with a reminder that, for the ancient Jews, "every second of time was the strait gate through which the Messiah might come" (1969b: 255, 263, 264).

The "Theses" have fed my imagination since I first read them ten years ago. They seemed both to anticipate and to sum up my own ambitions and desires as a Jewish scholar with their articulation of the links among the imperative of memory, the Jewish faith in redemption at any moment, and the secular revolutionary impulse. But, as I have said, there is a danger, an inherent falsification, in stopping at this level of identification. First, the articulations of the messianic imagination in Jewish tradition are extremely varied. To the extent that they focus on the restoration of a remembered past, that past is the period of national glory when the Temple stood in Jerusalem, not, as the critic Michael Loewy suggests, an original, Edenic, classless society (Loewy 1985). When Jews throughout the centuries spoke of the ingathering of the exiles, they certainly were not thinking only of exiled memory. Also, although there certainly is a universalist side especially in the prophetic writings about redemption, it is misleading to suggest that Jewish communities throughout the centuries were "the only [particular group] which gave credence to the program of universalization" (Bauman 1988: 50). Both the Christian Church and the Jews, in different ways, included in their programs for redemption universal recognition of their particular theologies.

Second, the imperative of memory in Judaism is not limited to overtly messianic motives, unless we accept uncritically Gershom Scholem's contention that Jewish messianism has compelled the totality of Jewish life to be lived "in deferment" (1971: 35). For Jews memory has also worked to plaster the ruptures in collective existence caused by repeated catastrophe and dispersal. It has been essential to the everyday continuity of a people who cannot rely on a linkage of blood and soil — so much so that when the attempt is made to substitute an organic identity for an anamnestic one, as in Israel, the outcome at times seems no more than genetically Jewish.

Jewish memory certainly does include resistance to domination in the name of a messianic conception of justice. It is not clear that this aspect can always be neatly separated from other modes of relation to the past: from nostalgia, a formalized longing for a patently constructed past; from panchrony, the sense of identification with prior generations experienced by "traditional" Jews; or from historicist empathy, that esthetic of obliterating the present that Benjamin denounced. To identify too neatly Benjamin's conception of the revolutionary power of memory with the place of memory in Judaism, therefore, would be to ignore the actual dynamics of the collective that has preserved for us the anamnestic resources of the Jewish textual tradition.

VI. The Scholar's Nostalgia

My own motivation to begin working in Yiddish ethnography was grounded in a profoundly nostalgic aching to know how life had been experienced in the pre-World War II East European Jewish *shtetl* communities and in a desire to share the language of those communities. My first researches—which resulted in a collection of excerpts from first-hand memoirs by Polish Jewish survivors (Kugelmass and Boyarin 1983)—were done under the spell of an impossible fantasy of doing participant observation fieldwork in the *shtetl*. Surely such fantasies are common to ethnographers and historians. Perhaps they may help explain Benjamin's famous technique of montage, of which he writes, "The work must raise to the very highest level the art of quoting without quotation marks. Its theory is intimately linked to that of montage."[3] The montage may be his solution to the problem of writing about a time in which he has not lived, without falling into the twin illusions of Olympian distance and total identification.

Whether we want to or not, however, anthropologists and historians work within a framework of motivating images of omniscience and of identification. Thus, drawn by my desire (as I conceived it) to make some contact with those who bore memories of the living *shtetl* world, and by my desire to know Paris and thus afford myself intellectual confidence, I arrived there with my wife, Elissa, in September 1982. My work with the immigrants focused largely on the fragmentations and disruptions that, more than anything else, have characterized their lives. Benjamin's work, in large measure, had taught me whatever I know about how to work with fragments. Much of his personal history and the history he studied overlapped with the events and forces that shaped the lives of the immigrants. Thus Paris became a Jewish-exilic chronotope where I met Benjamin and the immigrants. At moments, I was able to see where the cone of faded light cast by nineteenth-century modernity mingled with the nostalgic glow of the imagined *shtetl*. As small children living in the aftermath of World War I, many of the immigrants had been torn away from smaller Jewish communities and taken to the major industrial centers, or had spent their entire childhood in the cities. The destruction of those communities so soon after the emigration to France fixed forever the nostalgic image of home.

VII. Memories of Communism

Yet the fragment of their story that most fascinated me was the immigrants' relation to the Communist movement, to which so many of them had been loyal for decades. This relation encapsulated the problem of the links between their Jewishness and their identification with all of humanity, and between messianism and revolution. Most striking, their disillusion with Communism and failure to realize Zionism had left them in an ideological quandary remarkably evoking "the postmodern condition." They had gambled the grand narrative of the Jewish contract with God for secular dreams of redemption, and they had lost. Now, in their old age, they were busy inventing a much more personal and contingent narrative of their own lives.[4]

Communism was important to Walter Benjamin as well. I think that for him, as for the young, hopeful, proletarian immigrants who had nothing to lose, Communism represented a sort of horizon of redemption—a promise of totality overcoming not only the isolation of the individual but the isolation of particular groups of human beings as well. It was an ideal that also afforded the dangerous luxury of a degree of intellectual certainty—whether the certainty of eventual victory or the certainty of defeat. Benjamin wrote in 1929 that the "Communist answer" was "pessimism all along the line . . . unlimited trust only in I. G. Farben and the peaceful perfection of the air force. But what now, what next?" (1978: 191). Over the course of the 1930s, in fact, his confidence in this pessimistic answer was shaken. During those same years, on the other hand, the majority of recent Polish Jewish immigrants to Paris were reading the new Yiddish Communist daily, *Di naye presse*. Many of them remained loyal readers until the great breaking point after the Six-Day War, at which point a great number of them—already aged—defected en masse and became Zionists.

My point is not simply to tag Benjamin and the immigrants at different points on a time line with respect to their involvement with Communism, or to suggest that we can determine objectively why that involvement ended earlier for some than for others. Rather I am trying to bring out the easily forgotten point that at least some of the working "masses" and the dissident intellectuals were actively involved, in different ways, with similar responses to the crisis of their times. More urgently, I am trying to relate one contemporary answer to that crisis—Communism—to Benjamin's "aesthetics of redemption" (Wolin 1984) and to the problem that I and the immigrants have faced in trying to construct a coherent account of their lives, to construct, that is, a memory for them.[5]

For Benjamin, a criterion that must be added to Marx's vision of communist society as the ultimate resolution of conflicts among persons and between persons and nature is that for "a redeemed mankind [the past has] become citable in all its moments" (Benjamin 1969b: 254). Benjamin asserts elsewhere, however, that this criterion could only conceivably be fulfilled through the vehicle of "God's remembrance" (1969a: 70), in which neither Marx nor the immigrants had any faith. Scholars disagree about where Benjamin's hopes lay by the 1930s, but at least one of his goals in articulating this criterion must have been the avoidance of hubris by historians working in an unredeemed world. In the notes for the Arcades project Benjamin makes another comment on the link between messianism and history: "The authentic concept of history is a messianic one. Universal history, as it is understood today, is the business of obscurantists" (1983-84: 36).

By "universal history" Benjamin meant histories of the world written from a bourgeois, imperial perspective. But the critique may be applied to the mechanistic brand of Marxism dominant at that time. This has consequences for our understanding of the immigrants' ideological situation. They had been told, and believed, that the "Jewish question" would be settled with the coming of the revolution. This was one of the most tragic effects of the "obscurantist" universalism of prewar Communism. But to oppose to that form of universalism a so-called messianic conception, as Benjamin did, implies a concern with the lived history of all individuals and self-identified human groups, not just the Jews. Certainly Benjamin's linking of revolution to the messianic irruption is consistent with the Jewish "concept of re- demption as an event which takes place publicly, on the stage of his- tory and within the community" (Scholem 1971: 1). Yet for Jews throughout the centuries, any benefits accruing to suffering humanity from the advent of the Messiah were incidental to the redemption of the Jews. For Jewish Communists, on the other hand, the redemption of the Jews would be subsumed within the redemption of humanity.

VIII. Wandering toward the Light

Benjamin's study of the material and ideological form of Paris in the nineteenth century is linked to my ethnography of twentieth-century immigrants in at least two ways.

The first is that Benjamin documents the prehistory of the immi- grants' residences and workplaces. Benjamin remarks that the poet Charles Baudelaire—a major focus of the Arcades project, an arche- type for Benjamin of the *flâneur*, the idle and perspicacious observer of the crowds the arcades attracted—had at least fourteen different addresses between 1842 and 1848. These included the Quartier du Temple, the Ile St.-Louis, Saint-Germain, Montmartre, and Répub- lique (Benjamin 1983: 368). Temple is near the center of the Parisian textile industry, which the immigrants were so centrally involved in; Montmartre, or at least its slopes, was one of the major areas in which they lived; and the drab Place de la République is the epicenter of the part of Paris where all the Yiddish immigrant organizations are still located. Although the arcades certainly represented a bourgeois ideal, many of those still existing today are located not far from these tradi- tional working-class neighborhoods or are occupied by the textile and clothing shops the immigrants worked for and then sometimes owned. So to some extent the Arcades project details the prehistory of the space the immigrants would someday inhabit. But, contrary to that, there is also a fascination in Benjamin's work with Baudelaire and other nineteenth-century Parisian wanderers, with unsettlement, that echoes both his own uncertain immigration and the multiple home- lessness of the immigrants—who are bound in incomplete and unsat- isfactory ways to Poland, to France, and to Israel.

Second, the immigrants' own history—what attracted them to Communism and, to a lesser degree, what drew them to Paris—was shaped by Paris's situation as a beacon of Enlightenment, liberty, and progress in the decades before the immigrants were born. The Jewish Enlightenment, the Haskala, came later in Eastern Europe than it had in France or Germany, but it flourished when it arrived. The same was true of the Jewish workers' movement. Both looked to Western Europe, in part, for models of what they could accomplish and become, for the possibilities of their own liberation. And apparently internationalism really was the order of the day in Paris at a certain time. We may understand a bit better the immigrants' belief in the solidarity of all working people when we read Benjamin's quote from a text published in 1863: "The political opinion of the working class in Paris is almost entirely contained in their passionate desire to serve the movement for the federation of nationalities" (Benjamin 1983: 257).

Yet Benjamin was actually more interested in the nineteenth-century bourgeois imagination. Rather than resting at the continuity of working-class culture, it is worthwhile asking how that earlier bourgeois lifeworld compares to the mind-set and experience of these Polish-Jewish immigrant workers in the twentieth. One distinction can be made immediately: however much their dreams of redemption may have been mixed with ambitions of getting ahead as individuals, the immigrant workers had less opportunity to realize them in the years immediately before World War II. Thus, Benjamin writes about the rise of the private individual and private space: "living space becomes, for the first time, antithetical to the place of work."[6] Since many of the immigrants did piecework at home, they were not able to indulge in this antithesis. For them, social life was not separate from production.

This point can be extended. Benjamin is concerned with changes in the process of production, but his history of modern interactions with the world of things tends to begin with images or products already produced. His draft entitled "Paris, Capital of the Nineteenth Century" begins "Most of the Paris arcades are built in the decade and a half after 1822. The first condition for this new fashion is the boom in the textile trade" (1978: 146). Benjamin's focus on the material life of the commodity is related to his failure to mention the immigrants who were actually producing the textiles in the 1930s, while Benjamin was doing his study.[7] That production was the back of the mirror reflecting the cosmopolitan image of Paris.

Immigrant workers had little time, space, or money to enjoy commodities in private. But they could window shop, whether in the outmoded arcades or the *grands magasins* that replaced them. I suspect that part of what drew the immigrants to Paris — part of what fed their image of redemption as it related to their everyday world of work — was the lingering image of the arcades as an embodiment of the bourgeois utopian allegory of shelter from nature and, by extension, from history. Since Paris was a center of both production and consumption, the arcades and department stores must also have fed the workers with a vision of a redemption that properly belonged to them, since they had made it. This might have been expected to drive an unquenchable revolutionary urge. But immigrant workers in the clothing industries were hardly in a position to determine the strategy of the French left. And in any case, there was another, entirely contradictory lesson that this vision could impart. If commodities provide redemption, then there was hope that the capitalist structure that produces them could assume a benign form, without the necessity for class struggle.[8] Benjamin quotes one such nineteenth-century vision:

Riches, savantes, artistes, prolétaires,
Chacun travaille au bien-être commun;
Et, s'unissant comme de nobles frères,
Ils veulent tous le bonheur de chacun. (Benjamin 1983: 256)

To this painless vision of utopia corresponded the magical shelter of the arcades. These were early pedestrian malls, enclosing what formerly had been open streets.[9] The analysis of the arcades as an overcoming of the distinction between interiors and exteriors, or as a world brought inside, is a recurrent theme throughout Benjamin's project. He quotes a contemporary source:

"The arcades, a rather recent invention of industrial history,"
so says an illustrated guide from 1852, "are glass-covered,
marble-panelled passageways through entire complexes of
houses whose proprietors have combined for such
speculations. Both sides of these passageways, which are
lighted from above, are lined with the most elegant shops, so

that such an arcade is a city, even a world, in miniature."
(Benjamin 1969a: 146-47)

Elsewhere he writes of another artificial world, his surroundings while
he was doing his research:

> These notes, which deal with the Paris arcades, were begun
> under the open sky—a cloudless blue which arced over the
> foliage—and yet are covered with centuries of dust from
> millions of leaves; through them blew the fresh breeze of
> diligence, the measured breath of the researcher, the squalls of
> youthful zeal, and the idle gusts of curiosity. For, looking
> down from arcades in the reading room of the Paris National
> Library, the painted summer sky stretched over them its
> dreamy, lightless ceiling. (Benjamin 1983-84: 2)

That entry was placed in the folder Benjamin labeled "Theoretics of
Knowledge, Theories of Progress." This description of the scene of
research according to nature tropes might be described as Benjamin's
allegory of reading. More pertinent here, placing the description of the
arcades as a world next to the description of the Bibliothèque Nation-
ale illustrates the link in Benjamin's thought between theoretics of
knowledge and the theory of progress. When both are approached by
citation and allegory, we see how both involve the search for mastery
of nature—whether through enclosure, as in the arcades, or through
mimesis, as in the library.

In fact, Benjamin extended the image of the arcades as a world to
describe them as the *universe* domesticated: "the arcades, which are
both house and stars" (1969a: 157). We can connect that domesticating
nineteenth-century impulse to the imperial state, which sees itself
as the rationalization of space and the culmination of history, as
Benjamin claims: "*Empire* is the style of revolutionary heroism for
which the state is an end in itself" (ibid.). *The* end in itself, that is,
providing all necessities and obviating all other ends. This prospect of
safety and prosperity may have been attractive to the new immigrants,
most of whom had experienced the deprivation and dislocation of the
First World War as small children in Poland. Even their political involvement in France did not simply represent an ongoing commitment to embattled outsiderhood. In their new country, which boasted
a large, indigenous, and well-integrated Communist Party, Commu-

nism was not only an expression of faith in revolution—it was also a way of becoming French.

To emphasize this would suggest the transformation implicit in the word *passage*. On the contrary, Benjamin emphasized that the arcades were really about *not* passing through, about stopping. He presents them as representing claims of a premature attenuation of history, the end of change, the obviation of contingency in a kind of Saint-Simonian utopia. Susan Buck-Morss explicates Benjamin's insight that such fantasies are linked not only to commodity fetishism, but also more potently to "the original promise of industrialism. . . . to deliver a humane society of material abundance" (1989: 274), a magical transcendence without conflict. Most of the immigrants seem to have combined faith in revolutionary workers' solidarity with a desire to get ahead by gradually increasing the benefits they received from their own control of production. Those two motives were combined in the Popular Front, whose inevitable collapse helped set the stage for the collaborationist Vichy government.

Those immigrants who survived the war came to place much more faith in personally getting ahead than in universal redemption. After the war, they "became French" through being successful in business and through having French children. Their changed fortunes are easily explained by the contrast between the prewar depression and the extended period of expansion after the war and by the fact that they were almost all granted French citizenship after the war.

On the other hand, the persistence of the immigrant organizations into the last decade of the twentieth century testifies that they have remained a community of memory. The sharp contrast between their prewar struggles and hopes, the disaster that befell them from the late thirties until the end of the war, and their relative postwar success should give us pause. Isn't the Common Market another arcade? Commercial utopias—the arcades, the *grands magasins*, the Common Market—all relegate the discontinuous memory of the oppressed to the back storeroom.

Overcoming both historical chance and human exposure to the vagaries of nature, they also, paradoxically, hark back (nostalgically?) to times and places where contingency was suppressed and the relation between humanity and nature was conceptualized as eternal return.[10] In its pervasive modern form, "the myth of eternal repetition of the same . . . [is] created . . . by the limitless ambition of capitalism to structure a 'normal' everyday life devoid of politics" (Rolleston 1989: 21).

IX. Passages in the Field

The surface mood corresponding to the myth of recurrence is boredom. . . .
Benjamin equates boredom with waiting.
Rolleston (1989: 18)

I equate boredom with the worst sustained suffering I, a member of a relatively privileged class in our society, have ever experienced.[11] I also connect boredom — or rather my determination to break out of the cycle of eternal repetition in public school and college — to my desire to become an ethnographer, hardly a practical career for a bright young American these days. But the anthropologist's romantic search for exotica has justifiably been criticized in our reflexive years of a shrinking American empire. And to the extent that the ethnographer's stance may be compared to that of the *flâneur* — the idle observer, denizen of the boulevards and composer of newspaper *feuilletons*, who was such a key figure in Benjamin's portrait of Paris — the comparison constitutes an implicit criticism of the presumptions of ethnography. Benjamin cites, with the notation "regarding the legend of the *flâneur*," the following excerpt from 1858:

> With the help of a word I hear in passing, I reconstruct an entire conversation, an entire life; the tone of someone's voice is enough for me to attach the name of a capital sin to the man whom I've just bumped into, and whose profile I've caught a glimpse of. (Benjamin 1983: 542)

The *flâneur* and the ethnographer have similar pretensions. They presume to comment on human affairs as if watching amusing creatures from the heights, and at the same time they *are* those creatures, passionately involved in human affairs. Don't ethnographers advance their own aims by attaching psychological complexes, kinship structures, cosmogonies, and modes of production to people they hardly know?[12]

Benjamin's own description of the *flâneur*'s work habits also reads

in retrospect like a burlesque of the rhythm and self-justification of
ethnographic fieldwork:

> The assimilation of a man of letters to the society in which he
> lived took place in the following fashion. On the boulevard he
> kept himself in readiness for the next incident, witticism, or
> rumor. There he unfolded the full fabric of his connections
> with colleagues and men-about-town. . . . On the boulevards
> he spent his hours of idleness which he displayed before
> people as part of his working hours. He behaved as if he had
> learned from Marx that the value of a commodity is
> determined by the working time socially necessary to it.
> (1973: 29)

The ethnographer in me wants to reply, a bit too hurriedly and heart-
ily, "Yes, indeed! Gossip is our stuff in trade. And isn't it natural for us
to try to match our working schedules to those of the workers, the
common people with whom, after all, we identify, even though we
seem to be bourgeois?" We, reflexive anthropologists, are all too
aware of the ideal touted in an earlier generation of the ethnographer
as no-place (literally Utopia!), like Spengler's "civilized man, an intellectual nomad, [who] becomes again pure microcosm, absolutely
without homeland and spiritually free, like the hunter and the shepherd were in body" (Benjamin 1983: 970).

Now here's a curious point. Perhaps anthropology, in its fascination with the hunter and the shepherd, was responding not only to
what it was creating as Civilization's Other, but also to what it saw as
the physical analogue of Enlightened intellect. Which would help explain, at any rate, why anthropologists have been so slow coming to
write about their own everyday lives or those of other "civilized"
people. Yet Benjamin, rather than indulging in standard exotica, insisted that "we penetrate the mystery only to the degree that we
recognize it in the everyday world" (1978: 190). This brings anthropology back to a different heart of darkness, to the place where imperial anthropology begins. It brings us to the anthropology of Europe.

X. The Ethnography of Things

Benjamin isn't usually thought of as an anthropologist—perhaps be-

cause most Benjamin criticism has been done by philosophers, historians, and literary theorists. He himself, however, believed that
through the mediation of things it was possible to achieve the understanding of others' motives that characterizes the best cultural anthropology (even though he struggled against "empathy"). His unique
version of materialism—his profound respect for the artifacts of human culture—has been analyzed by Michael Taussig as a critical appropriation and valorization of the concept of commodity fetishism.[13]
Benjamin identifies this literal materialism with the ethos of anthropology: "The true, creative overcoming of religious illumination . . .
resides in a *profane illumination*, a materialistic, anthropological inspiration" (1978: 179).

It would be easy to read *anthropological* here as meaning merely secular, as the straightforward opposite of religious belief. But clearly
Benjamin does not have in mind a simple functionalist debunking,
since he retains the possibility of "illumination" and "inspiration." He
proposes that we see things neither as divested of spirit nor as contain-
ers of spirit in a dualistic sense, but rather as being constituted by the
sum of all the lives that have touched them and that still live in them.
Recognizing those lives in things is anthropological inspiration.

Benjamin sought an analogy for the quality of that inspiration in
the moment of waking from a dream, when we are still caught in its
world yet able to reflect on it. He stated the liberatory goal of his Arcades project: "This [presentation of history] deals with waking from
the nineteenth century" (1983-84: 10). When I think of the immigrants' dilemma—having abandoned Jewish tradition for a dream of
secular, universal redemption that in turn abandoned them—it tempts
me to suggest that my ethnography deals with waking from the twentieth century. This temptation is reinforced by an extraordinarily helpful comment by Buck-Morss:

> Benjamin proposed . . . that the *Passagenarbeit* provide a visual
> reconstruction of past history in fragmentary details. They
> would shimmer before the reader like the flash thoughts of
> memory, and the ghost that haunted their ruins in the present
> was the ghost of a failed revolution, the unfulfilled dream of a
> classless society. (1989: 146)

In her monograph on the Arcades project, Buck-Morss details the *se-*

ries of failed revolutions punctuating nineteenth-century French history: 1830, 1848, 1870. Polish Jews in Paris are also haunted by the ghost of failed revolutions. One—the first French Revolution—succeeded in instilling a concept of human rights, but left a continuing dilemma in its insistence on the abandonment of all particular identities. The second—the Russian Revolution—failed to become a world revolution, failed to liberate the Jews, failed to liberate its own people. The third—the Zionist revolution—has so far failed to establish a just order in its own country, or to realize a territorial solution to the predicament of Jewish existence.

XI. Remembering the Modern

But to stop at this parallel between the Arcades in the nineteenth century and Polish Jews in the twentieth would simply be to repeat Benjamin. I can't get away with that, since we still haven't woken up from the nineteenth yet. Although it is tempting to think of our own time as characterized by a concatenation of failed revolutionary hopes (1968, 1989), we thereby risk slipping into our own form of the eternal return of the same. That will hardly solve our problem. As the French Communist poet Louis Aragon threatened, in his own surrealist ethnography of the Paris arcades: "Death to those who paraphrase what I say" (Aragon 1971: n. 89). He might have written this as a prophecy: those who are content with paraphrase (not at all the same thing as citation!) will die.

Benjamin somehow intended to speak to whatever our predicament might be. He wrote: "Each epoch not only dreams the next, but also, in dreaming, strives toward the moment of waking" (1969a: 161-62). The alternatives to waking are continued sleep and death. While Benjamin focused largely on capitalist myth—that is, continued sleep—he also regarded the choice of death—suicide—as one of the most characteristic signs of modernity (1973: 75-76). There is something not quite postmodernist about Benjamin's association of historical insight with impending disaster. Benjamin here is not ironic or playful, perhaps because he is writing before the greatest disaster yet has come to pass. He writes of a sensibility that is surprised at the continued existence of the everyday world, of the feeling (quoting Leon Daudet, the author of *Paris Vécu*) that this world is "predestined for a catastrophe or several, meteorological or social" (Benjamin 1973: 85). On the next page he cites the insight that Paris could be destroyed like the great cities of the ancient world as the inspiration for a classic account of Paris in the second half of the nineteenth century.

The catastrophe Daudet had written of came soon after Benjamin wrote his notes. Perhaps Paris attracted me, as it attracts so many others, because in it survive both aspects of tradition and aspects of modernism. Not that Paris is impervious to change or oblivion; the arcades were of no use as a hiding place from history when the Vichy police came to round up Polish Jews. And even the "normal" forces of development, of course, have their destructive aspect. The Passage de l'Opéra, which Aragon describes in the first half of *Paris Peasant*, was destroyed as he was preparing his description. Decades later he explained:

> I had taken the precaution of choosing a landscape that would
> very quickly become unverifiable for the simple reason that
> the passage was about to be demolished in favor of an access
> way to the Boulevard Haussmann. . . . If that is not quite
> what really happened, that is still the way things turned out.[14]

Of course all things do eventually pass, and people too die sooner or later. But change comes so fast in our time that each generation soon comes to seem outmoded, in need of rescue . . . perhaps we might say in need of translation. For years, while I was writing my dissertation on these Polish Jewish immigrants and putting off revising it for publication, I think I regarded their history as unrescuable. Somehow their predicament—those who had been Communists having broken too late in favor of a sterile Zionism, those who had always been Zionists never having realized the call of their own ideology, since they stayed in France—always suggested to me that they had come to a dead end indeed. On the other hand, I was committed to presenting them with at least one account of their own history to which they could cling while still alive and that they could share with their children. And I needed that history too. I had come to them, in fact, seeking another link to the world of my own grandparents, trying to understand better why that link had been severed. Benjamin, who fought the tyranny of fashion by focusing his critical energies on the recently "outmoded," understood this need quite well:

The prehistoric impulse to the past—this, too, at once a
consequence and a condition of technology—is no longer
hidden, as it once was, by the tradition of church and family.
The old prehistoric dread already envelops the world of our
parents, because we are no longer bound to it by tradition.
The world of memory breaks up more quickly, the mythic in
it surfaces more quicky and crudely, a completely different
world of memory must be set up even faster to oppose it.
(1983-84: 7)

Benjamin is making a radical suggestion here: that nostalgia fills, in a
crude and opportunistic way, a need for an image of the past that can
no longer be satisfied by older techniques of memory and transmission. The phrase *prehistoric impulse* is uncomfortably reminiscent of *in-
stinct* and *drive*, and should certainly give us pause when applied to
such a complex linguistic function as memory. This point would
probably be a useful focus for continued discussion of the Arcades
project, since it is inseparable from Benjamin's rationale for the
project's political efficacy. The Arcades project was, at least in part, a
technical experiment aimed at finding a poetics of memory that would
simultaneously fill the need called forth by the "prehistoric impulse"
and also help us to awaken from the nightmare of class society or, as
Rolleston states, "to write the prehistory of the world crisis of the
1930s in such a way that its posthistory, the language of an awakening
from the nightmare culmination of commodity capitalism, would become a reality" (1989: 13).

What is the fate of that project? Certainly the revolution hasn't
come. And, instead of a messianic moment of awakening, Polish Jews
in Paris who were born before the 1930s and survived World War II
have chosen to reinvent—albeit critically—their shared cultural origins, and thus survive. Yet instead of silencing their revolutionary histories, they continue looking for ways to knit those histories with
their memories of their parents and their hopes for their children.
"The verdict on our dreams isn't in yet," the immigrants told me in
effect. "We're not dead yet. It's up to you. It's up to us."

XII. Instead of an End

These are some of the lessons, or perhaps warnings, I have been given by Walter Benjamin and by Polish Jews in Paris. All of them revolve around the need to acknowledge the passionate desire for totality and the simultaneous need to resist it.

In criticism, we are warned against the desire for a *rebbe*, a master whose dicta are all citable and consistent. This desire has led critics to attempt a purifying identification of Benjamin either as a Marxist or as a "theologian," or, more imaginatively, as a perfect transcendent incorporation of both of these inspirations. The last option is hard for me to resist. But to spend too much of our passion in wonder at his ability to predict the crisis of his time might lead us to miss the clues he could offer us to facing the crisis of our own.

In ethnography, as in memory, the desire is for a total account. When I was writing the ethnography as a dissertation, I was most powerfully under the sway of this desire, since it was then that I was most anxious to exhibit mastery. The immigrants' struggle to shape their lives retrospectively across and through a series of disasters, and Benjamin's fragmentary illuminations, may not have been enough to enable me finally to produce the long-awaited postmodern ethnography. They did help make it possible for me to acknowledge the partial nature of my knowledge and yet *to write*, that is, to contribute materials toward the reinvention of memory and community.

In Jewish identity, the desire for totality can lead toward attempts either to reify or to dissolve Jewish distinctiveness. My Paris fieldwork left me with an enormous respect for the political commitment of the immigrants and a conviction that their secularism had cut them off from the possibilities of both retrospective and prospective Jewish continuity. The challenge I am left with is the creation of a Judaism that is both anamnestic (bridging time) and universal (bridging space). Such a Judaism cannot be founded on a prior distinction between "religious particularism" and "secular politics" (Buck-Morss 1989: 250).

In the politics of history, the desire may be to present a monumental tradition of the oppressed. This urge can tempt us to mask the process by which that tradition becomes in turn a tool of oppression. Whether this results in an inability to see the power of past suffering fueling the ruthlessness of today's oppressor or in an inadequate care to see that those freeing themselves from oppression today do not become oppressors tomorrow, the danger is the same. Benjamin's characterization of this danger as "the threat [to tradition] of becoming a tool of

the ruling classes" (1969b: 255) is inadequate, since the events encapsulated in the tradition long outlive passing class structures.

Today class privilege and oppression are still powerful, but the
boundaries and characteristics of different classes seem more elusive
than ever, and we have little active hope of a global overcoming of
those destructive injustices. We're not waiting for the revolution.
We—historians, anthropologists, critics, politicians—should not think
of ourselves as prophets in training. Our training rather is in permitting the past to confront our blinders with its own account of the
present. As Benjamin writes, in a final quote that I cite in turn,

> By the time we come to discover that things are at a given
> juncture, they have already changed several times. Hence we
> always perceive events too late and politics must always
> foresee, as it were, the present. (1983-84: 27)

That would be quite an achievement. It might not bring the Messiah, but at the end of the twentieth century, enabling the species to
expect to survive would suffice.

Four

Jewish Ethnography and the Question of the Book

Beyond the valorization of native knowledge, beyond even the lesson that anthropology, too, is a cultural system, there is more to be articulated about the relation between the cultural practice of anthropology and the cultures that anthropologists practice on. The comparison of the treatment of certain themes in anthropology with those by people in cultural settings widely removed from the origins of modern anthropology is one way to investigate this relation (Borofsky 1987). My approach here is rather different. I attempt a critique of certain unspoken fundamentals in professional anthropology through references to the Jewish textual tradition—a tradition that is intimately related to the Christian textual tradition out of which ethnography more immediately arises—and to the situation of Jews who have lived in or near the centers of world power within which anthropology has been produced. This Jewish tradition has resurfaced, albeit greatly transformed, within postmodern theory. Making explicit its critical potential vis-à-vis the assumptions of ethnographic practice might, therefore, help to demystify and invigorate the contemporary practice of anthropology by revealing a particular manifestation of the link between knowledge and power. It should also help to explain why Jews have until quite recently been marginal as subjects of ethnographic study.[1]

I will launch the essay with a fragmentary discussion of Stephen Tyler's book *The Unspeakable*. Tyler himself is adept at the postmodern techniques of close, multiple, and playful reading, and therefore I do no violence by relying on strong readings of selected brief fragments from his work. The book is first of all relevant as an ambitious account of textuality and orality in anthropology. Tyler's understandings of the written and the spoken are unselfconsciously grounded in the Christian tradition, thus enabling me to show more clearly what happens when we bring the Jewish voice in. Furthermore, Tyler articulates a nexus between orality and textuality on one hand, and time and space on the other, that is extremely relevant to my concerns. He writes:

> It is a commonplace though many-named fact that there are two modes of integration, one a metaphor of space, the other a metaphor of time. The former is a static image of simultaneously coordinated parts, an objectlike structure, while the latter is a dynamic sequential relation of parts. Since Plato, at least, these modes of integration have been correlated with different modes of discourse, the sequential with narration and the simultaneous with argument or exposition. Plato's distinction between rhetoric and dialectic reflects this correlation, for dialectic in discriminating genera and species creates a taxonomy, a static and spatial image of reason which the syllogism merely recapitulates. In modern discourse analysis we have a similar contrast between the sequential and temporal formalisms of Propp and the simultaneous and spatial formalisms of Lévi-Strauss. Significantly, both Plato and Lévi-Strauss subordinate sequence to simultaneity. The indices of time—sequence, cause, consequence, and result are dominated by images of space—inclusion, exclusion, hyponymy, and the syllogism. (1987: 80)

It is hard for me to know what Tyler would say about this passage. Is he iterating a truth or unveiling a misconception? The former interpretation can gain support from linking his term *commonplace* to his prefatory plea in favor of a repressed "*common*sense world" (xi: emphasis mine) and from his binary assignment of time to Propp, space to Lévi-Strauss (and to Derrida; see p. 42). The latter reading, on the other hand, can also draw support from his antispatialist dissection of Derrida, for if the fact he is referring to is common*place*, presumably he would find something in it that needs to be demystified.

My general concern here is with the sentence fragment "fact that there are two modes of integration." These two modes do not exist simply; they are constructed and naturalized, and I want to see them as such. I will begin, then, by discussing a spatializing discourse to which I am hostile but whose beneficent intent I am making some modest effort to comprehend — that of academic area studies. I will end by discussing a temporalizing discourse to which I am drawn, but whose mystifying silences need to be made audible — a reading of the Jewish Bible that privileges textual identity to the virtual exclusion of the necessary spatial dimension of everyday life and collective identification.

My specifiable interests here are threefold. The first is my academic future as a Jewish anthropologist and an anthropologist of Judaism; I articulate this viewpoint in order to create a choice beyond what seem to be the existing options either of representing myself as being a specialist in an "area" that is not recognized as such and that indeed is properly not an area, or of abandoning my professional relation to a particular group of people in favor of a focus on "pure theory." The second concern is the general status of Jewish ideas in elite intellectual discourse; they should be neither ignored nor patronized. The third is the well-being of the Israeli Jewish and Palestinian Arab peoples. A critical approach toward the spatial and temporal grounds of ethnic identity is highly relevant to a better understanding of the construction of those two nations and of the conflict between them.

The index to Tyler's book confirms the gap between these concerns and the current theoretical/critical discourse in anthropology. There are no references there to Jews, Hebrew, Israel, or midrash, that genre of rabbinic interpretive literature that works largely by interweaving fragments of the biblical text and that has recently attracted considerable scholarly attention (see D. Boyarin 1990; Hartman and Budick 1986; Handelman 1982). The Kabbalah is mentioned in the text (p. 180), but it is not indexed, nor is the Zoroastrianism to which it is coupled. The one reference in the index to "Bible (postmodern ethnography and)" directs us to Tyler's statement that

> the hermeneutic process is not restricted to the reader's relationship to the text, but includes as well the interpretive practices of the parties to the originating dialogue. In this respect, the model of postmodern ethnography is not the

newspaper but that original ethnography — the Bible
(cf. Kelber 1983). (ibid.: 204)

The book Tyler refers to — Werner H. Kelber's *The Oral and the Written Gospel* — is a painstaking and insightful account of the transition from oral traditions to written texts in the Christian accounts of Jesus' sayings and life (see also Kelber 1989). But the Gospels are not what I usually have in mind when I think of the Bible, and it is not obvious that the same relation between orality and textuality obtains in the canonical Jewish books and in the Gospel. That Tyler himself identifies "Bible" and "Gospel" is further suggested by his Pauline paraphrase, "the letter of ethnography killeth" (1987: 99). It is easy to understand why this phrase is a powerful one for Tyler, since the ethnographic situation in which the oral dialogic of fieldwork is transformed into a monologic ethnography is so often roughly concomitant with the actual disappearance, the "death," of indigenous oral cultures. And yet we need to beware of this antigraphic prejudice, which Tyler shares with Paul: "If the apostle's thought is perceived as a theology of language, affirmation of the oral power of words and aversion to written objectification lie at its core" (Kelber 1983: 184). Kelber does indeed say that "an oral language deconstructed by textuality undergoes a kind of death" (ibid.:185). But he has also taken care not to evaluate the former as superior to the latter (16), does not believe in an evolutionary progression from one to the other (184), and cautions against the very search for origins (xv). The Bible I will be writing about here in its relation — critical or potential, but *not* original — to ethnography is other than the Gospel and, in fundamental ways, that which the Gospel constructs as its Other.

Note that Tyler is doubly validating the Gospel-Bible, both as the original of ethnography *tout court* and as the proper model for postmodern ethnography. Tyler's Bible is both the way ethnography was "originally" done and the way ethnography should be done. The indexing of the Gospel as *Bible* and as model postmodern ethnography, along with the absence of any Jewish references, suggest that for Tyler the relevant textual-interpretive sources of ethnography are generally Christian. The intimate link between missionary accounts and early ethnographic reports certainly reinforces this suggestion. On the other hand, there is the natural objection that so many modern pioneers in cultural anthropology (Mauss, Boas, Durkheim, Lévi-Strauss) were Jews. The issue, of course, is more one of social motivations and implicit frameworks of understanding than of the overt ethnic or religious affiliation of any particular scholar. Two observations can be made about the apparent contradiction between the Jewish personal origins of these pioneers and the Christian hermeneutic origins of anthropology as a whole.

First, all these Jewish scholars stand, as "assimilating" Jews, in an apologetic relation to the modern nation-state that is curiously analogous to the relation of the early Christians to the Roman Empire. Jews in post-Enlightenment Western Europe felt obliged to prove their loyalty to the new nation-states, and many of the secular scholars among them (Durkheim perhaps most notably here) did so by helping to elaborate the legitimating ground of liberal state structures. The record of the church fathers' relations with imperial Rome demonstrates a similar concern for compatibility between Christian loyalty and loyalty to empire and a corresponding dissociation from the particularist and rebellious Jews (Greer 1986: 121-22). The analogy is even more poignantly ironic when we consider that these secularist, modern, Western European Jewish scholars were, like the early Christians, "free to exploit the universalist aims of the religion from which they had sprung" (ibid.).

Secondly, identifying ethnography as profoundly (not essentially) Christian does not mean that its history is unrelated to Judaism. In fact, as I will discuss more fully later on, a major source of ethnography's logic of Othering is the early Christian encounter with Judaism.[2] What came to be normative, orthodox Christianity did not simply reject the Hebrew Scripture in the way the Gnostics did. Instead Christian hermeneutics were largely bent toward "the transformation of the Hebrew Scriptures so that they may become a witness to Christ" (ibid.: 111), a task made infinitely more difficult by most Jews' rejection of that "witness" (120). Here—as in the case of Marx's essays on the Jewish question or Lenin's confrontation with the Jewish Workers' Bund in 1903—the Jews stand as the test case for universalizing theory, which fails to deal adequately with a stubbornly distinctive group. But equally interesting, we are talking about a process of Othering that is simultaneously inter-"ethnic" and intertextual. Thus in a historical and not only metaphorical sense, the history of Othering is a history of reading; a crucial early moment in ethnography is the hermeneutic, intertextual encounter between the Christian Bible and the Jewish Torah.

I am hardly an authority on Christianity, although I am doubtless shaped by its cultural heritage more thoroughly than I could possibly be aware. Indeed it is impossible to imagine ourselves without the superethnic, individualized universalism elaborated in Christianity. Here, however, I am attempting to identify some of the mystifications inevitably entailed by the institutionalization of that universalizing thrust. One mystification perhaps linked to the early Christian ideal of a community whose members are linked *not* by history but primarily by faith is the idea of an abstract, undefined, yet nevertheless universally human common sense. Here Tyler, for instance, becomes wonderfully polyvalent. On one hand he generally valorizes common sense as one in a series of repressed, presumably liberating values, decrying "the triumph of logic over rhetoric, of representation over communication, of science over common sense, of the visual over the verbal" (1987: 170). Immediately afterward, however, he historicizes common sense, and undoes his own claims for its universal value: "These visual arts . . . are . . . historical emergents within a structure of common sense, and being thus relative to a cultural tradition cannot function as universals capable of constituting a fusion of all cultural horizons into a single integrated whole" (ibid.).

On this latter point I quite agree.[3] But it is instructive that despite this insight, Tyler feels constrained also to argue positively for the value of common sense. This obsessive sense of the need for a language of value that is both localizable and transcendent has been traced by David Lloyd to Kant's *Critique of Judgment*. It is superficially ironic that an anthropologist, of all scholars, should replicate this mystifying, universalizing move, since

> [for Kant, the process] constitutive of the public sphere of common sense . . . is formally identical with that which the human race undergoes in the movement from the primitive immediacy of gratification characteristic of "the savage" to the interest in "universal communication" characteristic of civilization. (Lloyd 1989: 38)

Yet what other choice does Tyler have, since he presents himself as accepting fully the poststructuralist dismantling of all given identities, all particular grounds of subjectivity, while still aspiring to "speak the language of resistance to all totalizing ideologies" (1987: xi)?

One might demand that Tyler situate himself culturally, whether as a member of an ethnic group or a participant in academic life or in any number of other possible ways. But to identify simplistically with any given collective might be in fact to succumb to a certain kind of total-izing ideology. Thus merely asserting that anthropologists (and other secular scholars), *too*, belong to particular and given collectives, to "cultures," or mapping one's identity and interest uniquely onto one's "own" culture, is an inadequate response to the problem of the scholar's specific identity. That would roll back what, through our self-interro-gation, we have accomplished toward undermining the lingering notion that "a culture" can be fully described and analyzed as a thor-oughly coherent and self-referential system. Anthropologists know this mathematic criterion of completeness and elegance cannot possi-bly be applied to their work at present, since the groups they study are contingently construed entities whose group identity inevitably entails blindness and exclusion. Nevertheless we (I speak from field experi-ence) are not only intrigued but sometimes made to feel helpless or incompetent by the apparently anomalous, by that which does not fit, by the inexplicable, or by that which can only be explained through reference to a past that may be overly complex or inaccessible. The creative response to this anxiety is an account that conceptualizes but does not totalize, that conveys patterns of meaning without pretend-ing that any group can be in control of all of its meanings, that distin-guishes between struggles for integrity and illusions of isolation. This is not an original insight on my part, yet it bears reformulation. It ap-plies both to the ethnography produced and to the ethnographer's view of the people written of, since the residual felt need for a com-plete and authoritative description of a spatially discrete and integral culture is closely linked to a lingering notion that authentic cultures are and should be whole and discrete (Thornton 1988).

The neurosis behind the occasional sense of helplessness I referred to may be described as an obsessive tendency toward spatial categori-zation. This tendency is evident in what, borrowing the approach of Lakoff and Johnson (1980), might be called a CULTURE IS SPACE metaphor. That metaphor is reflected, for example, in standard ethnographic titular forms from earlier in this century, where the prepositions generally refer to location: *Magic and Witchcraft among the Azande, Coming of Age in Samoa*. Tyler draws an appropriate connection between this spatializing tendency and the illusion of "an imaginary whole consisting of logically implicated parts" (1987: 194–95). This esthetic-political link between space and wholeness carries through to what the academic discipline calls area studies, in whose realm spatial metaphors also control our standards of professional competence and authority.[4] Not only museum exhibitions but also plans for academic staffing in departments of anthropology are often organized according to such "areas" of ethnographic concentration, which are in turn articulated with the programs of other departments and institutions. Many museums and departments resist strict areal organizations, perhaps for reasons similar to those articulated here.

The links between ethnographic spatialism and imperial politics are fairly transparent when we consider monuments in the development of the link between culture and place. The denial of history—of a chronological, developmental dimension—to the natives of North America, along with the denial of their proprietary rights, was grounded in a European settler ideology that saw the land as "virgin," unsullied by history (analyzed in Smith 1970). The United States "was defined primarily as a place," and its first "history," intriguingly enough, bore a title that combined spatialism with a particularist claim to universality: *The American Universal Geography* (by Jedediah Morse, 1797, cited in Jehlen 1986: 5).

A century later Professor Friedrich Ratzel, "the founder of political geography" (Gilman 1986: 216), published his compendium entitled *The History of Mankind* (1898).[5] The work includes colored frontispiece maps showing the territorial boundaries of such groups as the "Iranians and Kindred," "Germans" (including much of Scandinavia, most of Britain and Iceland) and "Semites" (the Arabian peninsula, much of North Africa, and, south of a narrow "Hamitic" belt, part of West Africa as well). This is not to suggest that Ratzel was unaware of popular migrations, nor indeed that he regarded racial natures as immutable: "Christianity grew up into a power capable of transforming races; to it, before all, the ethnographer refers the abolition of women's degradation, of polygamy, of slavery, of caste-separation" (1898: 548). The point, rather, is that in this scheme, every race has its place, and Ratzel knows what each race's place is (cf. Harvey 1989: 252, 275; Kern 1983: 224–25).

Nor is this a specifically German style or one limited to the classical age of imperialism, which is sometimes narrowed to the several decades before World War I. A standard reference used in my required graduate anthropology course in area studies was Clark Wissler's *The American Indian*. Wissler's introduction (presumably written for the original 1917 edition), read today, makes painfully clear the link between elegiac nostalgia for the vanished Other and the fact of exploitation:

> It is thus plain that we have before us one of our greatest cultural assets, the source of the most original traits of our present-day culture and a heritage upon which we may realize more and more. It behooves us, therefore, to systematize and extend our knowledge of this vanishing race whose life has been trampled under foot in the ruthless march of culture's evolution. (1950: xvi–xvii)

The notion of culture area that Wissler helped to formulate was intended as an ameliorative overcoming of the evolutionist assumption of a line of steady temporal progress from savagism to civilization along which peoples scattered over the world could be placed and ranked. Through the crucible of military uses during World War II, the culture area idea was linked to the paradigm of area studies that emerged after the war was over (Ford 1970: 7–8; Wood 1968: 404). The image of area studies has largely retained its relativist, humanist cast in expanding, liberal post–World War II American academia, and such reverses as area studies have suffered in the past two decades may reflect a decline in relativist empathy as well as a narrower conception of the profits to be gained from accurate knowledge of peoples at the "periphery" of the world system. But acknowledging the personal sensitivity of scholars such as Wissler should not keep us from acknowledging that their "concern for this vanishing race" is matched perfectly by an unquestioned need to grasp, to order the variety of Native Americans: "Some mode of classifying these many groups [is] imperative; for only in this way could the number of groups be reduced to the level of human comprehension" (ibid.: 219). The necessity, let alone the right, to engage in such classification and reduction is taken for granted. How else would a group (Wissler explicitly identifies "us" as Europeans) establish and legitimate their control of seized territory than by pinning the Other to a map? This does not mean, of course, that maps per se are in some way illegitimate, only that we must be aware of how their making serves legitimation.

The groundwork for such a critique of this spatialism in anthropology is laid in Johannes Fabian's *Time and the Other* (1983). His essential point is that the use of the present tense in ethnographic description reinforces a cognitive framework according to which those described are "out there," congealed in an unchanging, bounded panorama. According to Fabian, this stylistic convention further reinforces the prejudice that European scientific persons exist in time, in history, while those persons properly studied by anthropology exist only in culture (that is, so to speak, in space).

The ethnographic student of Jews is immediately confronted with the need to work against this learned neurosis. In its extreme form, spatialism doubly excludes Jewry as a collective from the purview of anthropology. First, the space in which Jews exist cannot be neatly delineated on the map, and they are still primarily defined, both internally and externally, as a minority wherever they live.[6] As a result, the ethnographic literature on Jews reveals confusion about their proper placement vis-à-vis established culture areas. This is ironically revealed in the first monument of Jewish ethnography written within an American academic context, *Life Is with People* (Zborowski and Herzog 1976 [1952]). The authors write that in the process of research, they had "the experience of discovering the existence of a whole at which we had not guessed" (ibid.:16). We may well believe that the research felt like a voyage of discovery, but the term masks the way their material was shaped into a distinctive image of the *shtetl*, one largely consistent with the village paradigm in anthropology. The authors could only make their point about the consistent and distinctive quality of Jewish culture throughout Eastern Europe by removing East European Jews from time (urban and modern influences are excluded from their account) and from space (the book presents a fiction of an idealized, atopic *shtetl* free from regional variations and non-Jewish influences). *Life Is with People*, that is, had to invent a Jewish culture area that was nowhere on the map.[7]

Second, the dynamics of Jewish collective identity are inconsistent with ethnographic spatialism. Certainly, particular Jewish communities may be (but, I submit, are not always) strongly grounded in the places where they live. To the extent, however, that Jews ground their collective, "national" existence in a specific territory, it is generally a territory (the Land of Israel) other than that in which they live. Doubtless the sense of a specific territorial origin and attachment to the Land of Israel is profoundly important to Jewish identity, even if it is not strictly "essential" (Davies 1982). In fact, recognizing this tension between local identity and "historical memory" (Shavit 1990) can illuminate the different possible groundings of various Jewish communities and bring home the point that the spatial factor, far from being irrelevant to Jewish culture, is both necessary and inseparable from time. Yet even when Jews do live on their "own" land, the collective is today still defined genealogically rather than territorially: Israel's Arab citizens are usually excluded from the common understanding of "Israeli" identity. Or, more precisely, within the ideology of Zionism there has been an attempt to substitute territorial identification for collective ritual practice and textual study while maintaining endogamy. This is a complex strategy with serious consequences for non-Jewish others—one in which ethnographic research is intimately involved. Hence Israeli ethnography is quite distinct (though not separate) from the Jewish ethnography I am trying to elaborate on here (see, for example, Goldberg 1977; van Teeffelen 1978; cf. Shokeid 1988).

There are several examples of Jewish ethnography sensitive to such nonspatialist issues as the negotiated identities of small groups of individuals or the reworkings of immigrants' collective memories (see, for example, Myerhoff 1978; Kugelmass 1986; Lapierre 1989). That the "space" for this kind of writing has begun to open up is evidence that anthropologists are not motivated solely by the same relations of power and knowledge that obtained in the colonial past. But it is still the case that there are never any academic job listings in Jewish ethnography (not that there necessarily should be). The areal demands for anthropological specialization are still largely determined by the state's political-economic investment in various parts of the world[8] or by its concern with various "minorities" within the state that need to be controlled and manipulated in various ways.

Beyond the negative critique sketched above, there are positive considerations for the creation of a distinctive Jewish ethnography. They are especially apt here because they relate to integral aspects of both Jewish cultural dynamics and postmodern thought about writing. Among these are textuality as an aspect of cultural practice; time, loss, and dislocation as inevitable determinants of culture; and the ceaseless traffic between oral and written modes of communication. All of these phenomena are exploited and resisted in the continuous work of reconstructing Jewishness, as in the postmodern work of searching for reasons to live and ways to communicate those reasons.

Perhaps the most relevant themes in postmodernist writing are the dismantling of the illusion of the omniscient, disembodied author and the concomitant blurring of genres. These themes are powerfully expressed in the work of the poet Edmond Jabès, whose work I find strikingly germane to current discussions in cultural anthropology. Jabès problematizes authorship and authority through the paradoxical joining of claims of memory and awareness of oblivion. His work blends "fiction and essay, theater and poetry, dialogue and monologue" (Caws, quoted in Motte 1990: 117). Ethnography requires similar responsible invention if it is to avoid both illusory totalization and elitist abstraction.

In my discussion of Jabès, I will treat him as a Jew—an identification he embraces while remaining removed from the Jewish community and its everyday traditions—and his writing as exemplary (though not "typical") of postmodern Jewish written expression. I will also treat him as an ethnographer, a risky move that is worthwhile because of what it reveals about the accepted genre boundaries of academic ethnography. Jabès neither uses Jewish references to score points in an academic philosophical debate nor attempts to portray a nonexistent cultural plenitude. His poetics of questioning is based on his need to know how to be Jewish when daily practice is an impossible answer. He was not born into that practice, and unlike some Jewish thinkers of comparable stature, he is neither willing nor able to choose doubt within observance.

Here I will discuss two passages from the first volume of Jabès's septology *The Book of Questions* with the intention of suggesting that Jabès's work can serve as one standard of rigor for the ethnographic challenge of recording Jewish culture while documenting its displacements. (Other models include the Talmud, the memorial books of Polish Jewry [Kugelmass and Boyarin 1983], and Walter Benjamin's Arcades project [1983].) Jewish ethnography, in turn, contains an as-yet-unrealized potential to make a unique contribution to an anthropology that aims to stimulate memory rather than sate the urge for nostalgia, to provoke contingent awareness rather than add to a static "store" of dominant knowledge (see Benjamin 1969a).

The Book of Questions is fundamentally about absences, displacements, the paradoxes of appearance. Yet it does not consist merely of language games. It does contain narratives, and at its heart there is an aching desire for the rabbis and the other persons Jabès names. Jabès, an Egyptian Jew, chose to write the story of two young European Jewish lovers who are victims of the Nazi genocide. Their story is told in fragments and, as in a page of the Talmud, most of The Book of Questions is commentary on or around their story rather than the plot unwinding.

According to a new study of Jabès's oeuvre, narrative concerns are in fact closer to the surface in The Book of Questions than anywhere else in Jabès's mature work. Yet already here fragments rather than wholes are the most urgent matter; "in its exaggerated discontinuity [the fragment] suggests the contrary, eliciting a nostalgia for unity" (Motte 1990: 104). Jabès's progressive retreat from the traces of realist narrative are related to his struggle against fixed genres, especially the novel (ibid.: 118). Doubtless I myself am more drawn to The Book of Questions than to Jabès's later work for the same reason I became an anthropologist: I am easily infected by that same nostalgia for unity, which realist ethnography shares with the realist novel (see Clifford 1988a).[9] The Book of Questions, in its spare narrative, is for me close to the limit of intelligibility. As a rhetorically imaginative rather than theoretical interrogation of writing, it cannot therefore be dichotomized either as atopic "ethnography" or as unreflected "raw culture."[10]

Jabès reveals his awareness of the demand for narrative in his reluctant and guarded surrender to it. He names the father of the female Sarah thus:

(The lives of one or two generations of men may fill one sentence or two pages. The gross outlines of four particular or ordinary lives: "He was born in . . . he died in . . . " Yes, but between the scream of life and the scream of death? "He was born in . . . He was insulted for no good reason . . . He was misunderstood . . . He died in . . . " Yes, but there must be more? [. . . .] "His name was Salomon Schwall . . . He does

not remember his youth . . . He left his island . . . He went
to Portugal . . . His wife was named Leonie . . . " Yes, yes,
but there must be more.[. . .] "He died in a gas chamber
outside France . . . and his wife died in a gas chamber outside
France . . . and his daughter came back to France, out of her
mind . . . ") (Jabès 1976: 166-67)

All this is told elliptically, as if to put back in place even the names of
what was lost were in some way a desecration of its more profound
absence. Yet Jabès does not stint with names: there are perhaps hun-
dreds of named, invented rabbinic commentators on the pages of *The
Book of Questions*.

What right does Jabès have to these names? This question is one approach to an essential question for Jabès's critics (which is also a fundamental question for Jewish ethnography): the question of Jewish
specificity. He himself traces his profound implication in Jewish collective destiny to his forced exile from Egypt at the time of the 1956
Suez crisis (1980: 48). Strange phrase: a Jew exiled from Egypt!

Yet it is not any physical Egypt that he longs for in his poetry, although he constantly writes of the legacy of the desert that he carries
within him. Instead, his forced flight sparked the consciousness of his
desire for an impossible Jewish identity. Impossible because of two
conditions he places on it, both of which are unacceptable to the community of believers: first, his assertion that "the relation to Judaism is
strictly individual before it can, or wants to, be collective" (1986: 355);
and second, his question (which is really a tentative assertion): "What
if this difficulty in being wholly Jewish were the same as everybody's
difficulty in being altogether human?" (ibid.: 359).

And still he asserts his equal standing. The nonbeliever, too, "does
not hesitate a second to answer 'Jewish' to the question of his identity"
(ibid.). In another place, he seems even to assert that his style of questioning is more authentically Jewish than the work of those usually
thought of as "Jewish writers":

For the Jewish writer is not necessarily the one who charters
the word "Jew" in his writings, but the one for whom the
word "Jew" is contained in all the words of the dictionary, a
word the more absent for being, by itself, every one of them.
(1985: 28)

Passages like these lead Jacques Derrida to claim implicitly and with approval that for Jabès there is no ethnographic specificity to the concept of Judaism; rather, "the Jew is but the suffering allegory" (1976: 75). Berel Lang, working from the same reading, attacks what he sees as Jabès's mistaken assumption that awareness of alienation is the heart of Jewishness. Lang supposes that for Jabès, "Jewish identity is engendered primarily . . . by Holocaust" (1985: 200), and Lang proposes instead an autonomous and essential desire of the Jew to exist *as a Jew*. A third voice, that of Maurice Blanchot, comes to assert the coexistence of the rupture constituted by the violent attack in our time against Jewish existence and the "original rupture, which is anterior to history, and . . . which, expressing distance in regard to every power, delimits the interval where Judaism introduces its own affirmation" (1985: 48).

Derrida, Lang, and Blanchot all ignore what Jabès's focus on the nomadic, desert setting of Judaism should lead us to recollect: the story of Abraham. Estrangement from the self, or at any rate a double consciousness, is constitutive of Jewishness not because we persist only through being repeatedly rejected by others but because there was a time before the Jew was a Jew. Abraham becomes the first Jew when he leaves his father's ways and his father's house to follow an invisible God. Coming to be Jewish is coming to be Other. What is relevant here regarding the possibility of a distinctively Jewish ethnography is that Judaism contains the Other in its own genealogy, that is to say, its own imaginary. This does not mean, of course, that Jews are inherently any more (or any less) tolerant or empathetic than any other given group of people, nor that the potential I am pointing to is exclusive to Jews. Yet it is extraordinary as a model of an elaborately inscribed identity constructed in the awareness of difference.

This may help us to make sense of one of Jabès's many aphorisms: "There was memory before there was recollection" (1985: 32). Memory is natural, so to speak, in an unreflecting and "happy" flow of generational continuity, now available only as a horizon of absence. Recollection is the work of doubling back after the initial break, reconstructing, always retrieving and reassembling in new combinations fragments of the past that are the fragments of our selves.

The inaugural wound, the founding rupture, is not only a philosophical concept. I doubt whether it is appropriate to assert that "In

Jabès's universe, Jew and writer wander in a postlapsarian desert . . . [where] the book assumes the function of humankind's *ground*" (Motte 1990: 123). Motte's use of the word *postlapsarian* is misleading; the (Christian) Fall is not the same as the (Jewish) Exile, universal as Abraham's chosen exile may seem when conflated with the collective exile after the destruction of the Temple. Still the Jewish wound is not as metaphysical as the Christian Fall. It takes place in history and in ritual, constituting fundamental themes of what we call Jewish culture: the recollection of a lost homeland; circumcision; the lesson of child sacrifice commanded, obeyed, and then—I pun intentionally—prohibited in the nick of time.

I would argue further that although Jabès is haunted by the history of Jewish suffering, he is not afraid that he will be killed by others. In his austere insistence on the honor of the written word, he seems much more worried about his possible moral death at his own hand, as a writer and as a Jew. As Freud, in *Beyond the Pleasure Principle*, writes a legend of hardy consciousness encrusting the vulnerable unconscious, Jabès seems afraid of letting the name "Jew" encrust Judaism.[11]

Jabès is most thoroughly Jewish, most like the first Jew in his absolute refusal of idolatry, his unwillingness to let himself rest comfortably for a while at some oasis of reification. His refuge is the book, not as the source of answers but as the privileged place of questioning. Something—not nothing—is created in the process: a renewed possibility of the Jew in history. Derrida writes that "the only thing that begins by reflecting itself is history. And this fold, this furrow, is the Jew." Which is to say that the Jew—and here, I believe, we can indeed substitute *humanity*—creates identity in creating history. There is no raw stuff of history separate from articulated history, nothing out there that simply, objectively, "is" history prior to human conceptualization.

I think we can say, by analogy, that there is no raw stuff of culture ultimately separate from ethnography. Rather, ethnography generally entails an anterior (and more general) process of "raw stuffing," something that not only anthropologists do. Ethnography is a distinctive genre, it is historically localizable, and it is also a particular form of the technique of producing differences that constitutes culture. That is to say—in the case of Jews—that the ethnographic study of Jews is one way to constitute Judaism, and also that living Jewish lives in a non-Jewish world necessarily entails constant reflection on cultural differences.[12]

But such a formulation seems to evade obvious questions. Can Jewish ethnography be done by non-Jews? Can it be done by believing, practicing Jews well-embedded in identifiable Jewish communities? Is it "best" done by those, like Jabès, who are Jewish by origin and identification but marginal to the putative "Jewish community" in terms of their social position and their critical stance?[13] Derrida, again, would seem to suggest that this last is the case:

> We must be separated from life and communities, and must
> entrust ourselves to traces, must become men of vision
> because we have ceased hearing the voice from within the
> immediate proximity of the garden. (1976: 68)

But let's not answer too quickly. Wouldn't a positive answer in favor of this last option privilege both organic identification and scientistic distance? Wouldn't it mean, that is, that being fully at one with an organic community, neither individuated nor alienated, is the ideal situation—but that once having lost that ideal state, the only way we can learn to "see" is by separating ourselves from life (as if that were possible)? It is important to bear in mind that, whatever Jabès may write about the Jew as a type, he resists any implication that he is putting Edmond Jabès forward as the very model of a postmodern Jew: "Some people deduced that I had made the Jew into a writer, and all writers into Jews. Whereas I had simply taken the liberty to underline their common relation to the text" (1986: 368).

In the same essay, Jabès writes against the notion that wisdom comes from an impossible isolation from "life and communities," resisting the dissociation that Derrida seems to be prescribing as the solution to the loss of revelation.[14] Jabès writes instead, in a passage that might have been written by Aragon, or by Buber, or even, in a burst of inspiration, by a professional anthropologist defending the necessity for the ethnographic encounter with the realia of Jewish life:

> Hence it is in and through its relation to the profane that
> we can experience the sacred, not as the sacred, but as
> sacrilization of a profane giddy with transcendence, as the
> indefinite lengthening of a minute rather than as an eternity
> alien to the moment. (ibid.: 356)

The profane is the social realm. For Jabès, the sacred is to the profane as the individual is to the collective; hence his problematic assertion that "the relation to Judaism is individual before it is collective." Nevertheless there is for us no direct, personal experience of the sacred, only moments of expansion within the book where we meet each other. Thus I would like to stop briefly near the story of Nathan Seichell (Jabès 1976: 76–82). In this passage in the first volume of *The Book of Questions* Jabès seems to come closest to the nostalgic, communitarian, everyday-life-in-the-ghetto discourse of much of modern Jewish literature. That genre is hardly unique to Jewish writers; it accompanies virtually every nationalism, and its borders with humanist ethnography are fluid. In this passage, Jabès both celebrates and subverts this tradition. Indeed, if read from a certain angle, Nathan's story is quite funny.

The passage containing the story of Nathan Seichell begins in the middle of Jabès's aphoristic discourse about shadows:

> God rests in man,
> as man rests under a tree.
> And the shadow, by grace of God, is man
> in the tree, and tree in man.
> I could have been this man. I have shared his shadow.
> "Yukel, tell us of the shadow we have in common."

Hence it is Yukel, not Jabès and not "I," who will tell Nathan's story. But before that there is rabbinic commentary about shadows: " 'A shadow is never more than appearance,' he said. 'But we know that the world, each morning, scuttles itself to make room for appearance.' " Two claims, each necessary for the other to make sense, are thus made here: First, that there is a relation of shared absence (shared "shadow") that makes it possible to imagine the Other: "I could have been this man." Second, that the shadow is no less momentous for being appearance rather than world, commentary rather than book. Or rather that there is no primacy between appearance and world, commentary and book.

In the unnamed ghetto where this short drama takes place, Nathan Seichell is both there and not there, like a shadow. As if to counteract our accustomed notion of pride of *place*, Yukel tells us that Nathan's room, "the most beautiful," is "an abandoned nook, furnished by the

imagination." Yet "On Passover, he eats on silver plates with engraved borders, borrowed from the Cohn family which is, rightly,
proud of them." Here are items we can lean on: material culture, folk
motifs, ritual loans of prized possessions. Jabès knows what he is writing. He is skirting the edge of ethnography.

As if to avoid coming too close, the tale describes Nathan's disappearance limb by limb, "as if between two ocean waves." His sister,
watching, "is rocked by the waves, just as the faithful in prayer seem to
be standing, but are really on their backs." In this chain of associations,
the faithful "are, in fact, boats at the mercy of wind and sea." Thus, for
Nathan who drowns, for his sister whose heart "carried her out toward
the open sea," for the faithful who float, the ghetto is not so much dry
land, nor is it stable. It is not always where it has been. It is not always a
place. It is not defined from outside. "The ghetto was like an island, its
outline defined, through the arm of Nathan Seichell, by the inhabitants'
anger, stubbornness, faith, and love." Only those at risk of drowning can
shape themselves into an island. Therefore "every Jew drags behind himself a scrap of the ghetto, a scrap of rescued land where he takes refuge
when alarmed." Is Jewish ethnography the scrap of ghetto the ethnographer invents to drag behind herself?

And here, with reference to the book, we finally come back to Fabian's
implicit riddle about the possibility of dialogue when ethnography is
part of a relationship of unequal power wherein one writes and the
other is written. There is a relation between the attempted silencing of
Europe's Jewish other and the imperial process within which, as
Fabian's subtitle puts it, "anthropology makes its object." Part of the
fear projected onto the Jews, and hence part of the mania to burn them
along with their books, stemmed from the insult of having within
Europe a people who commanded the power of their own books and
who maintained textual dialogue within them (Gilman 1986).

By the same token, there is a relationship between the questioning
of ethnography that Fabian's book is part of and the reintroduction
of Jewish themes, buried for centuries, into postwar European
thought. As Susan Handelman notes, while Jabès joins a distinguished
series of post-Enlightenment Jewish "readers" in European secular
culture, he is "the first to openly recognize and celebrate the renewed
'Judaization' of the book" (1985: 86). He has been tentatively desig-

nated "the poet of the contemporary world where dialogue and its dis-
contents are the (w)hole condition of meaning" (Fischer and Abedi
1989: 151).

But I do not want to use Jabès as a stepping-stone toward a claim
for Jewish hermeneutics as a new universal paradigm. Thus a question
must be articulated that cannot be answered fully here: Is the Jewish
ethnography I am pointing to truly unique? Insofar as the Jewish ethnography I am proposing is based on an ethic of questioning, it is
intimately linked to revival of Catholic, Islamic, and ancient Greek
traditions of interpretation and debate (ibid.: 150). Inasmuch as it is
based on a critical recuperation of repressed cultural traditions and on
giving voice to those elsewhere or previously silenced, it is perhaps
analogous to ethnography grounded in feminist criticism or in various
forms of subaltern experience (though we must note Spivak's conclusion that the subaltern *cannot* speak for herself [1988]). Still, Judaism is
extraordinary in the great emphasis it places on the desirability of all
(usually all male) Jews participating in the process of interpretive
meaning production through and around the book, and in its refusal to
declare the oral word prior to the written (see, e.g., J. Boyarin 1989).
Furthermore, inasmuch as the master tradition of modern ethnography grows out of Christian textual practices, the Jewish textual tradition
is pivotal precisely because Jews are an anterior, partly internalized and
partly repressed, other to the Christian West.

The contemporary European move toward "Jewish" styles of reading and writing seems, in fact, to mirror a much earlier move away
from cultural models based on the Christian transformation of Jewish
scripture. That earlier debiblicizing move is described by Michel de
Certeau, in a study of Joseph-François Lafitau, who in 1724 composed
a tome called *Moeurs des sauvages Amériquains comparées aux moeurs des
premiers temps*, and whom Radcliffe-Brown called "one of the precur-
sors of social anthropology." De Certeau explains:

> Lafitau takes care . . . to mark his distance from his
> comparatist predecessors, a fundamental distance. . . . Lafitau
> plays down the authority of the Bible because it is too
> 'localized' (there were societies before Israel), too 'positive'
> (general principles are needed), and too close to the 'fables,'
> whether savage or Greco-Roman, that he judged to be

'absurd.' *In the place of the Bible, there is a system.* (1980: 53; emphasis in original)

Here is, if you will, one "origin" of structuralism, or at least of "objective" social science (which simply means that the social scientist is not an object of study): a removal from the book, from narrative, and from history. This "theory has, however, the form of *a history which does not acknowledge itself*" (ibid.).

As de Certeau suggests, structuralism is inevitably contaminated by (its own) history. That history is linked to the narrative implied by the phrase "buried for centuries" I used in reference to Jewish reading. I am hardly competent to outline either account. But, to take up an earlier point, there is a close connection between the way early Christianity learned to construct its founding yet resistant Jewish Other through a narrative of temporal transcendence (see Moore 1986: 111), and the strategy of Othering in the nexus of colonialism and ethnography. As David Lloyd puts it, albeit without reference to Jews: "The ethical narrative of universal history that informs exemplary [bourgeois] pedagogy [and within which anthropology takes its place as moral instruction—J.B.] is easily envisaged as a secular transposition of the redemptive narrative of Christianity and clearly retains much of its temporal figurality" (1989: 51, n. 8).

The eventual failure of the Jews in Western Europe to be so redeemed (so to redeem themselves) is another aspect of the failure of "the ethical narrative of universal history." The most vicious potentials of liberal social science, born of secularized Christianity, were realized. The Nazis victimized Jews with a double ideologizing of science. On one hand, they exiled and condemned as "Jewish science" the suspect, subversive relativist physics. On the other hand, they claimed in the name of objectivist "anthropology" to have demonstrated the distinctive inferiority of the Jewish "race." Again, it seems clear that it was particularly threatening to Nazi racial ideology to find within Europe an "inferior race" that nevertheless was capable of subverting objectivism and racism.[15] Jews still have a stake in dismantling the legacy of objectivist and antireflexive scientism, whose effects, at least according to radical formulations, have not been so different outside Europe (see Said 1989b). The potential of an ethic of questioning in helping to accomplish this dismantling rests in the fact that it necessarily posits an Other who *can* answer in her own voice, and whose response is desired.

That this dialogue indeed *is* desired (and simultaneously resisted), at least in post-Holocaust, postcolonialist, postmodern, poststructuralist France, is clear from the centrality in contemporary French intellectual discourse both of the Jewish voice and presence and of the Jew as exemplary absent Other.[16] It seems fair to suggest that French thought today finds it needs to have recourse to Jewish ideas (or at least ideas it identifies favorably as Jewish) in order to keep its own tradition from collapsing (a danger dramatized by the concatenation of *posts*). Trying to understand this entails further distinctions, at the risk of reification, oversimplification, and chauvinism.

The tradition of Christian textual authority against which Lafitau rebelled was of a different character than the powerful midrashic element in Jewish reading. To the extent that it is possible to speak in gross terms of a difference between Jewish and Christian reading, this difference, significantly but not totally, is one between resistant and dominant reading. The Christian Bible itself is always a processed version of "rawed" material, a translation, a preselection from among the multitude of possible interpretations (although Christian readers through the centuries have often consulted with Jewish readers or the Hebrew Bible itself [see Smalley 1964]). Its prevalent interpretive mode—allegory—is structured so that a "native" reader of the "original" could not possibly produce the authoritative allegorical reading, as Gerald Bruns (I think unintentionally) explains:

> Allegory is . . . the interpretation of a text or corpus that has been resituated within an alien conceptual framework. Allegory presupposes a cultural situation in which the literal interpretation of a text would be as incomprehensible as a literal translation of it. (1987: 637)

In any case, "comprehension" (taking together, taking as a whole, placing), is much more a problem for the dominant position in any encounter of differences.[17] It is only conceivable within an intermediate semiotic realm, wherein the Other may be abstracted both from her own expression and from her direct impingement upon the dominating interpreter. The illusion of that intermediate, superior realm is sustained in structuralism by the denial or denigration of the letter and of history, and in the early official Christianity of the Roman Empire by the Augustinian denigration of the letter, the body, and sexuality (Pagels 1988).[18] Mentioning Augustine reminds us that he was a convert and that the search for singular, authoritative interpretations in early Christianity had to do not only with differentiating Christianity from Judaism, but also with setting bounds for the new community and attracting adherents from "outside" with the promise of access to Truth.

The Jewish Bible (whoever we believe its Author or authors to be, and, in most cases, unlike the Old Testament portions of the Christian Bible) is studied in Hebrew. This permits interpretation not only of the conceptual content of Biblical verses but also of the sounds, homonymies, orthographic variations, calligraphic ornamentations, and other features of the text that surpass our prejudice for a fixed and arbitrary linkage between sign and significance (see Dan 1986, especially 128-29). At the same time it does not entail the splitting of the sign from the signifier, or the interpreter from the text. Furthermore, while Judaism has hardly been free from internal and external ideological challenges (and thus from repeated orthodoxies), never until the Enlightenment was it predominantly shaped by a need for codification, catechism, and justification to the outside. Hence interpretive authority (unlike daily practice) need never be regarded within the tradition as univocal or irrevocably closed. (Perhaps this is why Jabès is drawn to Talmudic style rather than synagogue worship.) This is clearest, of course, in the characteristic rabbinic interpretive mode of midrash, wherein "it is *the whole dialogue* which is authoritative, not just the isolated interpretations that emerge from it," and whose task "is to keep open the mutual belonging of the text and those who hear it" (Bruns 1987: 632-34.) This midrashic, dialogic play of interpretations within the bounds of an implicit ethical framework is a model for a kind of Jewish ethnography that would not only be the ethnography of Jews. The approach I am proposing is Jewish not only in content but in form as well.

The proper strategy, therefore, might *not* be one that seeks to overcome the marginalization of Jewish studies within the discipline of anthropology, to establish Jewish ethnography as a bounded, separate field.[19] It may be more rewarding in the long run to explore the lessons for ethnography in the Jewish interpretive model of multiple and diffuse authority, of dialogue with and *through* a narrative, textual source whose potential meanings are never exhausted, and hence never fixed. Narrative—about Jews especially perhaps, but also narrative in general as a human faculty—keeps alive the "Jewish question" after genocide, but in order to stay *alive*, it must remain a question, as Jabès writes: "As you can see, this attitude is very different from one that says: we do not exist, I obliterate myself, thank you and good bye. No. I efface myself in order to go even further" (Auster 1985: 22).

Of course, going further simultaneously entails searching deeper within; as Jabès writes elsewhere, "freedom consists in going back to the sources." I do not presume to specify what Jabès's sources are, but in my reading, his exilic stance rests constantly in the shadow, so to speak, of the pre-Exilic image of functioning, everyday community described in the Bible (agriculturally based, temple-oriented, based on collective moral responsibility). At the same time, he refuses to let that image mask the absence of such community in the present. He refuses, that is, precisely the rabbinic substitution of ritual solidarity for material community.

Indeed, one brilliant recent reading of the Bible contends that it is a narrative of the necessary failure of the attempt to sustain an agricultural, territorially fixed society without falling into the trap of idolatrous, hierarchical organization (Berger 1989). That reading, however, concludes with the recommendation that rather than deluding ourselves once again with the notion that control over land can be harmonized with community, we subscribe to a "narrative of . . . exile [that] offers no expectation of return to its chronotopical referent" (ibid.: 136). The community thus yielded would be "the hermeneutical community, the community of textual desire" (ibid.). Echoing Jabès, Berger describes his place as "the textual home where all good landless Israelites still live" (ibid.: 119).[20]

Unfortunately, this prescription ignores both its own inherent elitism and the experience of Diaspora Jewish history. The only purely hermeneutical community that could possibly afford equal access to all would have to overcome the same hierarchical tendencies inherent in territorially based collectives. It would not only have to overcome fully the bars to interpretive access imposed on categories such as "women" (an effort that must be continued in any case), but more problematically, it would have to exclude or tyrannize those who are not apt or inclined to construct their identities primarily through read-ing. We don't have to return, as Berger does, to biblical history for instructive experiences in this regard. The collapse of traditional Jew-ish life in the modern period came, along with outside pressures, from a revolution against an elite rabbinical "community of textual desire." "Like monarchs or lords who identified (named) themselves through their lands" (Jehlen 1986: 16), the Jewish elite in exile named them-selves through their books. Yet they were unable to adjust their hermeneutics fast enough to maintain the loyalty of massive numbers of East European Jews.[21] Together with various competing secular movements, Labor Zionism most violently opposed this bookish Ju-daism, substituting for it a remorseless conquest of space (see Jean-Klein 1988). The disastrous consequences of that one-sided dynamic are in turn now becoming evident.

Hence neither "the book" in itself, nor "the land" in itself, is ade-quate to sustain the combination of moral exigency and historical con-tingency that, together, constitute Jewishness. Neither is dispensable. Whereas I began by criticizing what I see as an overemphasis on land and space as against time, memory, and the book, Michel Foucault believed that space has been devalued for generations, and that more dynamic use of "spatial, strategic metaphors" would effectively high-light questions of power (1980c: 70). Since time and space are both constantly being reinvented, we need to subject our inventions of them to constant questioning. Perhaps, right now, one thing we need is a sort of negative ethnography: we (not only Jews) need to know better what we have surrendered in our conquest of the land.

Five

The Other Within and the Other Without

*I would like to ask whether [the idea] that it is necessary to conceive the
Other as a radically separable and separate entity in order for it to command
our respect . . . is a useful idea. Just how other, we need
to force ourselves to specify, is the Other?*

S. P. Mohanty (1989: 5)

In an essay on the Enlightenment search for Atlantis as one possible
alternative to replace Biblical Israel as the origin of European civilization, Pierre Vidal-Nacquet notes that "to be autochthonous means
never having been instructed by an other; the theme is fundamental"
(1982: 58, n. 80). Though it certainly predated what we usually think
of as the period of Romantic nationalism, Vidal-Nacquet shows that
the Enlightenment included several attempts to locate an "autochthonous" European civilization in such places as Sweden or Italy. Representing competing national visions, on a larger scale they collaborated
in a project of "overcoming the Judeocentric vision of the history of
the world" (ibid.: 14). After 1679, when Olof Rudbeck first published
in Uppsala his *Atlantica*, attempting "to show that Sweden was the
cradle of history, that it was Atlantis and its capital Uppsala . . . virtually no one who borrowed the myth failed to refer to the proud
Swede" (ibid.: 19).

Most of us no longer believe in Atlantis. Most of us have overcome
the passionate desire to claim pride of origin for a particular ethnic nation. Many of us, in fact, have come to question the very search for the
origins of civilization. After the horrors of colonialism committed in
the name of civilization and the horrors of "autochthonous," blood-
and-soil Aryanism, the Enlightenment twist on Christian superces-
sionism has come into some question. In some quarters, in some

registers, beyond the question of origins, an explicitly Jewish voice has emerged in critical social thought, largely as a response to the apocalyptic eclipse of reason during World War II.

Yet for that voice to remain vital, to retain a connection to the memory of the cultural worlds it grows out of, it must be articulated with other emergent voices in the aftermath of colonialism and of triumphal modern progressivism. There are many such voices, offering an almost infinite number of points of initial contact. The choice, in this essay and elsewhere, may seem almost haphazard. So be it. We are learning to be less embarrassed at the traces of our own confused invention.

Here, at any rate, I will take two strong voices in cultural critique as starting points for comparing Jewish and postcolonial difference and the ways that ethnography has articulated or could otherwise articulate those differences. The first is several recent essays by Edward Said. In his article "Representing the Colonized" (1989b), Said responds to the various calls and proposed strategies for letting the voice of anthropology's object into the finished product of ethnography. Said insists that the anthropological project still remains trapped in a situation of dominance over its object. The Other, that is, remains outside, as she must in a neocolonial situation where power/ knowledge remains concentrated in the old imperial centers. Said believes that the imperial project, the control of the colonized world and the extraction of its labor power and material resources, was the most urgent task for white Christian ideology in Europe. The "interlocutors" of anthropology he is interested in are therefore the colonized and the formerly colonized. Nor will Said accept the simple equation of the colonized with other excluded groups, such as workers or women, whom he sees as equally implicated in enthusiasm for the imperialist project (1989c: 6). Though Said identifies the Eurocentric imperial vision as "the idea of white Christian Europe" (ibid.), nowhere does he direct his attention to those inside Europe who were not Christian. On the other hand, he is certainly right to suggest that

> hostility to Islam in the modern Christian West has
> historically gone hand in hand with, has stemmed from the
> same source, has been nourished at the same stream as anti-
> Semitism, and that a critique of the orthodoxies, dogmas, and

disciplinary procedures of Orientalism contribute to an
enlargement of our understanding of the cultural mechanisms
of anti-Semitism. (1985: 99)

Here, then, is one lifeline. Though Said's critique of the discipline of
Orientalism has been criticized in turn as monolithic (Clifford 1988b:
Thom 1990), it stands as a powerful model for the archaeology of cultural and biological racism in the service of nationalism at home and
colonialism abroad. The tendencies to essentialize Self and Other, to
buttress national collective identity with a fiction of majestic and pure
origins, to create grand schemata of cultural history that cloak themselves in the rhetoric of scientific authority but appear in retrospect as
ludicrously speculative—these were all practiced since the early modern period on various of Europe's Others, notably including Muslims
and Jews (Olender 1989). If the hangover of Orientalism—a rubric
that certainly includes expertise on Jews—demands from us a dissolution of essences, a complication and contamination of origins, that
demand calls to critical Jewish thought as well. Similarly, if the postmodern turn in ethnography is challenged by Said's insistence that the
object remains trapped by the scientific ethos of dominating comprehension, Jews as an object of ethnographic inquiry should be trapped
the same way. Or are they? I will return to this question toward the
end of this chapter.

   A second starting point is the distinction Gayatri Spivak draws between teaching as "information retrieval" and teaching as a politically
enabling critical practice. Thus, she says, teaching Indian history outside India is information retrieval, but doing so inside India is really
active *teaching*. Analogously, for Spivak teaching critical theory in
India is information retrieval; it's about "other people," whereas
teaching theory in the United States "is a critique of imperialist cultural politics" (1990: 91). The underlying assumption here is apparently that Indian students are not empowered to engage critical theory,
either to change it or to apply it dynamically within their own situation; for them it can serve only as a means to acquire academic legitimacy. Readers of Spivak's book will decide for themselves whether
they want to accept this dichotomy. It seems to preclude the possibility that scholars living and working in India might, through the common medium of the English language, have a critical effect on or

through theory, or that pretentious theory developed within the former colonial metropole could speak powerfully to those in the postcolonial situation. It is based, like Said's critique, on a spatial distinction that mystifies as well as reveals.

But the force of Spivak's distinction here should not be lost, nor should the reality of differential authority to "take on" theory be denied, nor should the distinction Spivak (like Said) makes between Others inside the metropole and the vast millions of the formerly colonized be minimized. Indeed, Spivak uses her recognition that "the stories (or histories) of the postcolonial world" are not the same as "the way the metropolitan countries discriminate against disenfranchised groups in their midst" (1989: 274) as a way to acknowledge that postcolonial intellectuals can be placed in positions of relative privilege vis-à-vis those "native" disenfranchised groups.

The analogous lessons for a critical Jewish ethnography are twofold. First, it is important to distinguish between the related aims of using theory to validate the study of Jews, to make their difference seem just as momentous as gender or colonialism (analogous to information-retrieval type legitimation), and of engaging theory toward the articulation of a postfoundationalist Jewish identity (analogous to the engaged critical practice Spivak promotes). Second, Spivak's clarity about the paradoxical position of the postcolonial intellectual in the metropole serves as a reminder that Jews, too, can be used as a privileged Other in ways that mystify both anti-Semitism and the larger system of domination of which it is an integral part.

Nevertheless, there are a number of reasons why these attempted analogies might seem irrelevant or forced. The first is the conventional geographical specification of the Other as being outside Europe or, since the nineteenth century, outside Europe and America (Baudet 1965; Fabian 1983; Barker et al. 1985; Torgovnick 1990; Mason 1990; Cheyfitz 1990; Campbell 1988). The title of Spivak's earlier collection of essays, *In Other Worlds*, reinforces this spatial organization, emphasizing by a pun the way the English *word* is situated outside England. Even if we immediately think of a metaphoric use of *world*—India and England as different cultural worlds—they are located along a spatial axis, they are "distant" from each other. The spatial difference emphasized by Spivak's title is reinforced by the cover illustration, a reproduction from a seventeenth-century Indian illuminated manuscript. It is only inside, in the text, that we read about Spivak's careful articulation of Marxist, deconstructivist, and feminist insights and that Spivak acknowledges her debt to Jacques Derrida for enabling her to live in other worlds (1987: author's note). Spivak, appropriately echoing Derrida's own discretion, says nothing about his Jewishness. She refers to herself by the official designation "non resident Indian"; what would it mean to call Derrida a "nonpracticing Jew?'

As inescapable as the emphasis on the colonized Other is, however, it ironically complements an ingrained repression of ethnography about the Other inside Europe. An instructive case in this regard is that of Richard Simon, a seventeenth-century priest, Christian Hebraist, and ethnographer of European Jewish communities. Simon was eventually excommunicated—not, apparently, for doing fieldwork, but for his argument against Bossuet that the Hebrew Bible as received had been falsified by the Jews after Jesus to remove the prophecies of his coming. At first there seems to be a contradiction between Simon's accusation of Jewish textual distortion and his sympathetic ventures into contemporary Jewish community life. But closer consideration suggests that, in the context of Church doctrine, his sin was consistent in both respects. Questioning the received text, Simon disrupted the work of Christian centuries that worked out the doctrine of Christian supercession. Articulating a view in which "Jewish communities come to life, are transformed over time and according to the places where they settle" (Olender 1989: 111; see also van Gennep 1920, Yardeni 1970), Simon upset the notion that since Jesus' time Jewish life and thought had been petrified. The Church, that is, had more or less dealt with the problem of its internal Jewish other by distancing that other in time, fixing her in the past. Simon threatened the temporal boundaries. Bearing his example in mind, and remembering that designating traits of cultural distinctiveness as "survivals" is another way to assure their death, we may hesitate to relegate the Jewishness of someone like Derrida to a mere "biography effect."[1]

Said's plausible insistence on imperialism as a *geographical* fact cancels out the significance of these temporal boundaries of domination: "Imperialism after all is an act of geographical violence through which virtually every space in the world is explored, charted, and finally brought under control" (1989c: 10). Said is correct, of course; but we are so accustomed to thinking of time and space as contrasting axes that this emphasis on spatiality tends to marginalize discourses of temporal Othering. We speak of distant times, but not of places long ago. Different places exist simultaneously, but different times do not exist in the same place—except in the minds and writings of extraordinary individuals such as Walter Benjamin. Thus, if the vast preponderance of Jews who resisted imperialism culturally or militarily and the vast preponderance of Jews who were victimized by imperialism are dead, rather than elsewhere, their relevance to the struggles of postcolonial people against (neo)imperialism seems impossible to discern. The question then arises whether those who are not in a position to be interlocutors (of anthropology, literary criticism, or any other form of contemporary critical thought) because they are dead cannot *also* be a source of critical discursive power. Where Spivak asks "Can the Subaltern Speak?" (1988), one item on the agenda for those who would revive a critical Jewish discourse is "Can the Dead Speak?" Again, while the intuitive answer is no, an underground tradition says that our lives depend on hearing them, while a new initiative in academic anthropology has begun to explore ways of relating to the Other through time (Ohnuki-Tierney 1990).

I consider Said and Spivak here because, largely thanks to their own efforts, they are now situated along relatively clearly established fault lines, or paradoxes, between excluded Otherness (he as a Palestinian exile, she as a nonresident Indian) and authoritative scholarly privilege. I am trying to explore an analogous fault line that has been occluded in several ways.

The first way is called assimilation. This is a misnomer, since it assumes an unchanging nature on the part of the non-Jewish majority, which Jews can approach if they have the will and if they are given the chance. The assumption was consistent with a liberal argument, enshrined in anthropology, that differences between groups were cultural rather than biological inheritances (Kirshenblatt-Gimblett 1987; Gilman 1986: 219). It should be clear that the dissolution of distinctive Jewish communities could only be conceived within a larger society that was itself dissolving, changing in unprecedented and unpredictable ways, and that the anxiety of this change fueled in turn the growth of both "cultural" and racialist anti-Semitism.[2] Still, even after the Nazi genocide, the critique of the Enlightenment remains incomplete inasmuch as Jewish assimilation is tacitly assumed to be the modern norm, while Jewish separatism and exclusion are regarded as odd holdovers from tradition.

Second—and surprisingly related to assimilation—there is the fact of annihilation. This obscures the Jewish difference in various ways. There are fewer poor Jews than there were in 1939, fewer Jewish radicals, fewer Jews who speak a nonstate Jewish language. Also, many people in Europe and America were so horrified by the genocide in their midst that, at least until now, anti-Semitism has been excluded from much polite discussion, and, as I suggested earlier, Holocaust memorials have taken pride of place in a postmodern culture of imperial guilt. Likewise, the Holocaust itself sometimes comes to be seen as the one really dreadful thing that has happened to Jews, effectively precluding serious cultural criticism of the situation of Jews before or after World War II, as when Renato Rosaldo notes that "the humor in Marx's use of anti-Semitic stereotypes does not make one laugh out loud, particularly not after the Holocaust." (1989: 191). The shadow of the Holocaust makes it hard, even for those like Rosaldo who understand the power of the past, to see how seriously we must think about the temptation to laugh at anti-Semitic stereotypes *before* the disaster (cf. Greenblatt 1990). Much as assimilation assumes a fixed and approachable non-Jewish culture, fetishizing the Holocaust assumes an undifferentiated situation before and after—whether that situation is seen as endemic anti-Semitism, in the Zionist view, or as "normal" tolerance, in the assimilationist view. Moreover, Rosaldo overlooks the basic problem with Marx's essay—the Hegelian view that the continued existence of the Jews is a scandal, a bizarre anomaly that must be explained away. By apologizing for Marx he effectively reiterates the objectification of the Jews and thus misses the chance to integrate a Jewish perspective within his model of "diversity."

A third form of occlusion is related to the formation of a Jewish state. Spivak may be a nonresident Indian, but I am not a nonresident Israeli—except in the Zionist dream. This does not prevent radical critics from making the paradoxical assumptions that (a) Jews can't be in a postcolonial situation because they are participating in a belated colonial venture, and (b) Jews are no longer a Diaspora people because they now have a "homeland." The first assumption places Israel outside the pale of legitimate "new nations"; the second implies that the "Jewish question" has been solved by the creation of Israel. There is a confusion here between the boundaries of inside and outside, between a positive emphasis on difference and a frequent presumption of unanimity among Jews.

Hence the double and linked thematics of this essay. The first dimension I am exploring is the contrast between the Other outside Europe and the Other inside Europe. My focus of course is on Jews, but the purview might well be extended in several directions. Peter Mason, for example, has considered the relation between the early colonialist representation of "Plinian" monstrous races in the New World and the construction of witches and the insane as explored by Foucault (Mason 1987). The problem with this analogy is that witches and the insane are understood in this paradigm as a reflexive effect of the self-constitution of civil society. Sartre notwithstanding, the scholarly consensus today holds that the continued existence of Jews cannot be reduced to an effect of anti-Semitism (Finkielkraut 1980; Friedlander 1990). Rather than pursuing this Foucauldian direction, it might be more helpful to consider under this rubric groups that have not yet been brought within the convocation of theory; one thinks immediately of the Romani.

Consistent with Spivak's spatial conception of cultural worlds, the boundary between within and without can also be the boundary between the collective with which one is conventionally identified and the presumptively alien collective Other. The older catechism of American anthropological practice held that only the Other without was a fit subject for research, since distance encourages objectivity; the notion was self-evident a few years ago, but seems almost bizarre today. At the same time work was being carried out in many rural backyards and national archives in Europe, often under the rubric of folklore.[3] The boundaries between ethnography of the Other without and folklore of the Other within were not necessarily rigid; thus the manual produced by a member of S. Anski's ethnographic expedition among the Jews of the Ukraine near the turn of the century was titled *Yidishe etnografye un folklor* (A. Rekhtman 1958). Long before Anski's expedition, however, the nineteenth-century German Jewish founders of *Wissenschaft des Judentums* (the science of Judaism) had formulated a way, through objectivist research modeled on colonial ethnological science, to maintain their Jewish identity while distancing themselves from their "primitive" contemporaries and forebears. Simultaneously they wished to purify Judaism of elements of folkloric "superstition," to separate out those universal elements that could inform a modern Judaism compatible with ecumenical liberalism. This is primarily a strategy of Othering in time, allowing identity to draw on identification with a heritage that now can be dispensed with. *Wissenschaft des Judentums* aimed, perhaps, at laying to rest "the savage in Judaism," and thus complemented the efforts of contemporary Christian scholars of ancient Judaism, who aimed

> to radically differentiate Judaism and savage religion [as] part of an ongoing attempt to protect the privileged status of Judaism, and by extension, Christianity itself. This motivation informed the work of both Jewish and Christian interpreters from the Enlightenment until the present day. (Eilberg-Schwartz 1990: 4–5)

Thus the scholars of *Wissenschaft des Judentums* doubtless shared with many scholars in the late twentieth century the assumption that the dualities they detected in the Bible—between culture and nature, human and animal, mind and body—were part of a shared Greek and "Judeo-Christian" mythology (Haraway 1989: 246). Christian and Jewish scholars alike studied colonized peoples as well as ancient Jews and were motivated in complex and semiconscious ways by shared images of the colonized savage and the superseded Jew. Furthermore, as Eilberg-Schwartz's emphasis on apologetics suggests, such scholarship could be a technique of self-defense, not only an aggression against the Other. Cultural folkloristics arose in debate with, and partly as a defense against, the rise of physical/racialist anthropology (Belke 1971).

In a fundamental way, the projects of studying the Other within and the Other without are linked by a shared goal: "our ways of making the Other are ways of making ourselves" (Fabian 1990: 756). But even this view reproduces a dichotomous logic. Self and Other, Jew and Christian, ancient and modern, within and without . . . It is a truism common to structuralism and deconstruction that we tend like our ancestors to produce our world in binaries. François Hartog notes that this pattern, which at first appears as the rule of the excluded middle, comes to seem not so much a rule obeyed by the narrator or procedures he deliberately adopts, as a rhythm, a beat which runs through the narrative. It appears that, in the end, in its efforts to translate the "other" the narrative proves unable to cope with more than two terms at a time. (1988: 258)

Or, as S. P. Mohanty puts it in the sentence I have used as an epigraph here, "just how other . . . is the Other?"[4]

All of the foregoing suggests an archaeological project connecting questions about the formulation of modern cultural anthropology and the problematics of modern Jewish identity. Clearly there is something buried there, and it may be accessible at several points.[5] This would help, for example, to explain the prominence of Jews in sociology and anthropology during the decades around the fin-de-siècle. Gyan Prakash has emphasized "the colonized's appeal to and affiliation with the subordinated selves of the colonizer" (1990: 405); doubtless the appeal and affiliation have been made from the other direction as well. My concern here, however, remains with the layers of topsoil overlaying that buried history. Why is it that the Otherness of Jews has tended to be occluded in Europe and America since World War II?

One reason, I suggest, is the hegemony of empathy as an ethic of the obliteration of Otherness. We might say that this occurs where humanism demands acknowledgment of the Other's suffering humanity, but where conditions do not allow the work involved in what Eric Cheyfitz calls "the *difficult* poetics of translation" (1990)—that is, where the paradoxical linkage of shared humanity and cultural Otherness cannot be expressed. In popular-culture representations of the Holocaust, the particular horror of the Nazi genocide is emphasized by an image of Jews as normal Europeans, "just like us." In fact we can only empathize with, *feel ourselves into*, those we can imagine as ourselves. Thus in the television docudrama *Holocaust*, the Jewish protagonists are a middle-class, German-speaking nuclear family. Conceivably, such representations might make viewers marginally more alert to anti-Semitism in the present, but they do not really expand the space of the Other.[6]

Where does "empathy" come from? Is it Greek, Christian, imperial, generally universalist, or all of the above? In a painstaking, though necessarily selective, study of the sentence "I am you," Karl Morrison has begun to sketch out a history of the concept. Although Morrison's references go back to Vedic texts, he argues that

> within Western culture, the sentence and the patterns of thought that it epitomized originated in ancient Greece. Neither sentence nor patterns of thought owed essential meaning or content to the other two fonts of the Western intellectual tradition, Old Testament Judaism and Roman thought. . . . True to that beginning, the sentence and its meaning retained their cogency among people who moved easily in the intellectual heritage of Greece, and who worked in inquiries of high abstraction, rather than the forensic and social inquiries in which both Old Testament Jews and Romans of the classical and postclassical periods most notably distinguished themselves. (1988: 27)

Morrison's scope is large, and he aims toward a redemptive critique, attempting to demonstrate the intellectual and ethical vitality of what his subtitle calls "the hermeneutics of empathy." Inevitably, therefore, he remains virtually silent about the repressive effects of empathy on those who remain beyond the pale. Thus, he provocatively begins his preface with a discussion of Fichte's call for the removal of the Jews from Europe, since they are a stumbling block in the path of European brotherhood (xii–xiii), but doesn't return to this issue except for the general caution that "The example of Fichte . . . does not let us escape from the question of how doctrines of harmony justified conflict and even persecution" (137).

Except for Christ, the individual who appears most often and most consequentially in Morrison's account is Augustine. In an extended review of Augustine's interpretation of the Jacob and Esau story, Morrison reveals (though he fails to state) how Augustine appropriates the figure of Jacob for Christian theology while simultaneously distancing the Jews. For Augustine, Esau represents carnality, Jacob spirituality; Esau the Jews and Romans, Jacob the Christians; Esau the earthly Adam, Jacob the heavenly Christ; Esau the reprobate, Jacob the elect (82–83). In Jacob's struggle with the angel, by contrast, Jacob takes on a double moral persona: "In his withered member, Jacob personified . . . Jews and bad Christians, people of carnal vision, whereas in his blessedness, he personified true believers." (83). We may well ask what has happened to empathy here; Augustine's treatment of the biblical narrative seems much more like an opportunistic appropriation of selected motifs to score points determined in advance. Especially noteworthy here, as elsewhere in Augustine, is the contrast between Jewish carnality and Christian spirituality (D. Boyarin forthcoming)—one of the prime figures that will be carried forward into the thematics of colonialism, with the Christian remaining in place and "the savage" being substituted for the Jew. Perhaps the Augustinian heritage can even be seen in the anti-Semitism of the idealist humanist Fichte: for spiritual empathy to take place, those who are trapped in base carnality must be removed.

But Morrison does not explore any of these suggestions. Doubtless he could not have achieved such a broad reopening of a long-neglected theme without the deployment of such selective blindness, along with strategic dichotomization. The latter is seen, for example, in the passage quoted above where he identifies empathy as Greek, not Jewish or Roman—once again, as if these terms referred to three noncontingent cultural worlds. For Morrison, the flaw in Western culture is the incomplete synthesis of the Greek theme "I am you" and the Jewish commandment "Love your neighbor as yourself." He attributes this failure to social structure—individuals' loyalties "to family, cult, class, party, nation, or state" (357). Curiously, however, whereas Morrison repeatedly emphasizes the aspect of domination inherent in metaphors of male empathetic acquisition and female reception, he has nothing to say about the role of power in the histories of the Greek theme and the Jewish commandment. He does not articulate what his account repeatedly suggests: that Greco-Christian empathy flowers within a situation of imperial triumphalism, against a Jewish ethics that works outward from particular identification with those who are closest to one.

We are left, then, with the impression that spiritual empathy is not a particularly Jewish theme and that it tends to be deployed from a position of relative dominance. It would be important to explore in detail the role that an implicit hermeneutics of empathy plays in ethnographic fieldwork method, especially in the practice of "participant observation." The assumption—much diluted now, of course, but still shaping our work—is that by doing what "they" do for long enough, the anthropologist can learn what it is like to be "one of them" and thereby earn the right to articulate the experience of the inarticulate, to write the experience of the illiterate.[7]

This strategy is not only relevant to the deployment of empathy in space. It also underlies empathetic historicism, the goal of sufficiently forgetting one's own context and sufficiently immersing oneself in a world distant in time that one comes to share the experience of the dead. Having seen the link between empathy and empire, we can better understand Walter Benjamin's insistence that "the adherents of historicism actually empathize . . . with the victor" (1969b: 256). Historicism implies control over the past, comprehension of all its aspects, confidence that it will not surprise us by coming to life in the present. In the triumphal view of universal history and unidirectional progress, the European can comprehend the spatially distant Other empathetically because the savage is contained in the history of civilization. In much the same way, present-day historians can comprehend the past because they have developed out of it. Thus the distinctions between the Other within and the Other without, the Other in space and the Other in time, collapse at the pinnacle of *modern* European imperialism.

What possible alternatives are there to the triumphalism of empathetic participant observation or empathetic historicism?

First, it is not the case that because there are problems with empathy, other strategies will necessarily be benign. Rhetorics that are grounded in the assumption of "radical alterity" do not necessarily encourage a respect for the right to live differently. Instead, they may permit a more solipsistic, less self-reflexive deployment of tropes of Otherness to suit selfish needs of the moment. We have seen something of this in Augustine's discussion of Jacob. François Hartog describes a similar case in Herodotus: When it is a question of the Greek identity, the Scythians appear as the opposite of the Greeks; when the Persians need to appear like Greeks, the Scythians are contrasted both to Greeks and to Persians (1988). They are available as an all-purpose topos; it little matters what they are "really" like. Lack of "empathy," then — the lack of any demand for an attempt to comprehend the experience of the Other — may feed into ethnocentrism.

Ethnocentrism is consequential both within and without the boundaries of the ethnic group. It is a powerful means of enforcing solidarity, often at the cost of repressing internal difference, and it legitimizes discrimination against those excluded from the group. I suspect, then, that we cannot blithely dispense with empathy, with some presumption that human experience is commonly approachable across the lines of difference (see Mohanty 1989). What we need to do instead, perhaps, is to reinscribe empathy more knowingly, with a critical awareness of the power relations and the tendencies to symbolic violence its usage implies. Isn't a measure of empathetic identification inherent in the idea of postmodern criticism? As I have come to understand it, *postmodernism* implies not a progressive supercession of the modern, but a critique from within that preserves the freedom of modernism while dismantling its progressivist pretensions to be the last and culminating word. Hence an eclectic diffusion of participant observation, the sense that we are always susceptible to the cultural systems we analyze, characterizes the prominence of criticism in contemporary elite culture. Everything becomes fieldwork.

Yet as sympathetic as I am to the postmodern turn, it frequently betrays itself in a hubristic rhetoric of accomplishment: *finally* we have realized that we are what we write, *finally* we have realized that the observer cannot be separated from the observed, *finally* we know that the monstrous Other is the monster in our minds . . . Postmodernism, that is, can betray the very opening afforded by Benjamin's remark that " 'the state of emergency' in which we live is not the exception but the rule" (1969b: 257). If postmodernism is at least partly characterized by the anthropological stance of participant observation, then, it is vital to explore the analogies within European cultural history to the insidious potentials of anthropology. This is one approach to finding the right questions about the relations among universalism, imperialism, and genocide.

I want to focus briefly on the case of Germany—not so much the German state as a machine for wielding power as the project of creating a national German collective identity. We have become accustomed, since World War II, to seeing the German state as a sort of beast whose violent tendencies must be kept in check. Perhaps, especially given the events of 1989 and 1990, we are coming to the limits of that frame of reference. It is particularly timely, then, to situate the project of Germany within various relations of selfhood and difference.

The juxtaposition of France and Germany, for example, reminds us of another dimension of internal difference, another relationship between Others within. The historical consequences of the rivalry of first Prussia and then Germany on one hand and France on the other are not to be minimized, even though they are localizable inside the imperial metropole. Indeed, this rivalry served effectively as a topos for rhetoric deploring intolerance among "equal races," which some liberal colonialists saw as blocking "the regeneration of inferior or bastard races by the superior races" (Renan quoted in Olender 1989: 87). Furthermore, consideration of Germany helps to destabilize the rigid geographical distinction between the imperial world and the colonized world:[8] Germany is within Europe yet has an ambivalent relation to empire, coming late to colonization and eventually seeking empire within Europe. Doubtless the fact that the Nazi genocide against the Jews was committed by German speakers, rather than by the rulers of one of the great modern European empires, has helped to obscure the relationship between colonialism and genocide. But these are larger questions than I am equipped to pursue.

My interest, following Sander Gilman's recent book *Jewish Self-Hatred*, is in the threat that Jewish linguistic difference within German-speaking lands posed to the creation of a German national identity based on a common language. Gilman traces in painstaking detail the attitudes of non-Jewish scholars in German-speaking lands toward the Jews, their language, and their books, starting with the sixteenth-century Christian humanist Reuchlin, who held that the Jews were not worthy of their own books and did not know how to read them correctly (1986: 42-44). Do we not hear echoes of Richard Simon, who would claim a century later that the Jews had actually falsified the Bible? Much of what even Christian humanists knew about Jewish classical texts was learned, of course, from converts, and much that converts wrote was in the form of virulent, scurrilous "exposés." Here is the dark side of the notion that the native is the one who truly knows; the convert's insider exposure of "the hidden language of the Jews" (as Gilman's subtitle puts it) is the demonic reverse image of participant observation. Later, in the period when Romantic and folkloristic nationalism flowered, the question of the holy texts ceded precedence to the search for a pure national vernacular. Yiddish came to be seen as a deliberate corruption and desecration of German, a secretive and lying code, and as a particular threat to the new pan-German political identity based on a standardized literary language (ibid.: 71 ff.). Hence the manic anti-Semitic insistence on the "Jewishness" of the language of nineteenth-century journalists writing in German. And, as is well known, German Jews in their chimerical quest for assimilation distinguished themselves carefully from their Yiddish-speaking past and their Yiddish-speaking cousins to the east. One way to accomplish this was to collapse the two, to *localize* the past outside Germany. As Gilman describes, the Jewish convert Gottfried Selig did this in his Yiddish textbook of 1792 by claiming that Hebrew words are used in Yiddish in ways

> so deformed that they appear to be parts of the Hottentot language. . . . Thus in the eyes of the formerly Yiddish-speaking convert, Yiddish moved from being a language of a "nation within nations" to a language of the "barbarian." But for the Jew, convert or not, these barbarians must be localized, like the Hottentot, in some remote geographic place to separate them from the image of the German Jew. Their locus is the East, specifically Poland, and the Yiddish-speaking Jew becomes identified with the Polish Jew. (ibid.: 99)

It is worth bearing in mind that in the late seventeenth-century, German speakers did not have a very direct ideological investment in "Hottentots"; they were simply a metaphor for distance and incomprehensibility. When Selig, a converted Jew writing in German about Yiddish invoked them, it was indeed the Other within that he was trying to exorcise — the Jew inside himself and the Jew inside "Germany." Here again, we realize that there is no justification for a global insistence on the priority either of the colonized or of marginal groups within Europe. What needs more attention is the interaction between the two in the dominant imagination.[9]

The need to set a boundary between "native" German Jewry and primitive Yiddish speakers became especially acute when East European Jews began migrating to Germany en masse, invading and unsettling the metropole much the way the Third World has come to work in Europe since World War II (see Wertheimer 1987; Kramer

1980). The great investment German-speaking Jews had in maintaining the distance between themselves and the immigrants doubtless helps to explain the degree to which many assumed that the Nazis would perceive the same distance, and thus spare them.

Here we are faced with the way a strenuous and sustained attempt to become the same came up against an Othering so violent that it resulted in annihilation. It is a good point to turn the ethnographic gaze back on Europe—not to study "folk culture" or ethnicity inside Europe, but to employ a *Verfremdungseffekt*, using the anthropologist's distant eye to see the most rarified ideas as culturally marked products. Perhaps the most general "idea"—indeed, one so pervasive that it has only been articulated recently in the process of critique—is the notion of Europe as the point of reference, the topos of the same, an idea that is inseparable from the idea of progress. The linkage of the two produces the notion of a progressive world history culminating in post-Enlightenment Europe, "universal history" à la Hegel. In some ways this picture of universal history, which was hegemonic until the middle of this century, has already come to seem strange under the combined impact of decolonization outside Europe and genocide within. In other ways it persists, sustained by the reification of memory and history as fundamentally different modes of relating to the past, with the Jews as a favorite case of a "people of memory" in opposition to history (Yerushalmi 1982, Nora 1989; cf., however, Funkenstein 1989a). The temptation to romanticize Jewish history in this fashion— ironically linked to a new validation of memory—reinforces the lingering assumption of a universal history that the Jews somehow fall outside of.

Although the mature Hegel supported the civil rights of Jews as part of his vision of civil society, as a young man he saw the biblical narrative as the origin of alienation. In his *Early Theological Writings* figures such as Noah, Abraham, Joseph, and Moses are responsible for the eternal and unchanging nature of the Jews, removed from history and the human community. For the young Hegel the Flood is the ur-event, destroying the organic unity of humankind with nature:

> It was in a thought-product that Noah built the distracted
> world together again; his thought-produced ideal he turned
> into a Being and then set everything else over against it, so

that in this opposition realities were reduced to thoughts, i.e.
to something mastered. (1977: 183)

This alienated relation to reality is further developed in Hegel's
account of the history of Abraham. His leavetaking of Ur of the
Chaldees, his wanderings, the act of circumcision, his insistence on
paying for the field of Machpelah rather than accepting it as a gift, all
are seen as evidences of Abraham's rejection of the general human
community: "The whole world Abraham regarded as simply his opposite; if he did not take it to be a nullity, he looked on it as sustained
by the God who was alien to it" (ibid.: 187). Abraham's descendant
Joseph, acquiring viceregal power in Egypt, introduces legislation
whereby the subjects of the Pharaoh are brought into the same relationship to him as Joseph stands to his Idea, that is, the relationship of
slave to master. The diatribe continues, with Moses' role as liberator
being ridiculed and his giving of the Law regarded as merely the laying on of another form of bondage. In Hegel's summation, he criticizes the Jews' dependence on an unseen God and their inability to
worship beauty:

> The subsequent circumstances of the Jewish people up to the
> mean, abject, wretched circumstances in which they still are
> today, have all of them been simply consequences and
> elaborations of their original fate. By this fate—an infinite
> power which they set over against themselves and could never
> conquer—they have been maltreated and will be continually
> maltreated until they appease it by the spirit of beauty and so
> annul it by reconciliation. (ibid.: 200)[10]

Hegel may have later dropped the overtly theological language, but
contemporary Jews never fit into his scheme of providential world
history. So I come to a zero point, where the Jews appear both superseded by a post-Christian account of providential history and obviated
by a spatialist critique of imperialism that sees the population of Europe as an undifferentiated mass of colonizers.

It is time to bring in Kafka—a Jewish voice from the other side of the
abyss. Many of Kafka's texts challenge the genre boundary claims of
professional ethnography. They are produced on cultural border lines,

but not as "information retrieval." Kafka's ethnography of simultaneous Jewish loss and emancipation has much to teach us through the engagement evident in those texts.

The *Letter to His Father* is an obvious example. Several pages in the letter detail his childhood impressions of his father's Judaism, along with his retrospective analysis of those impressions. Kafka wants to understand how something that struck the child as utterly empty could have been significant to the father, and in the process he sketches the experience of countless Jewish parents and children in the modern period:

> You really had brought some traces of Judaism with you from the ghetto-like village community; it was not much and it dwindled a little more in the city and during your military service; but still, the impressions and memories of your youth did just about suffice for some sort of Jewish life. . . . Even in this there was Judaism enough, but it was too little to be handed on to the child; it all dribbled away while you were passing it on. . . . The whole thing is, of course, no isolated phenomenon. It was much the same with a large section of this transitional generation of Jews, which had migrated from the still comparatively devout countryside to the cities. (1976: 79–83)

Here is a relation to the Other within that is quite different from Hegel's myth of eternal Jewish servility, but also quite different from the folklorism of the *Wissenschaft des Judentums*. The content of Judaism in the "ghetto-like village community"—removed from Kafka's Prague childhood in both time and space—is not restored, but only hinted at through the marks of its absence. Kafka neither exoticizes the traditional, rural Jewish Other nor attempts to obliterate the distance. The focus here is indeed on "the difficult poetics of translation"—and in this case, the translation of Jewish intimacy from the village to the city has failed.

The impression is confirmed in a fragment called "The Animal in the Synagogue" (Kafka 1961: 49–59), in which Kafka adopts the voice of a Jew in a small town, speaking perhaps to a visitor from the big city. The imaginary animal is described in some detail: "about the size of a marten," "pale blue-green in color," and so forth. It is located quite precisely within the architecture of the synagogue; like a child it prefers to stay near the women's section, but the beadle does not allow it to stay there. It is "more shy than a denizen of the forest, and seems to be attached only to the building." But the animal should know that soon it will be able to stay in the synagogue undisturbed:

> The congregation in this little town of ours in the mountains is becoming smaller every year and . . . it is already having trouble in raising the money for the upkeep of the synagogue. It is not impossible that before long the synagogue will have become a granary or something of the sort and the animal will then have the peace it now so sorely lacks. (ibid: 51)

But meanwhile, curiously enough, the animal in the synagogue only appears when the Jews gather for services, although it probably would like best to remain in "some hole in the wall" where it lives when no one is there. When it does come out, it is drawn toward the Ark of the Covenant,

> but when it is there it is always quiet, not even when it is right up close to the Ark can it be said to be causing a disturbance, it seems to be gazing at the congregation with its bright, unwinking, and perhaps lidless eyes, but it is certainly not looking at anybody, it is only facing the dangers by which it feels itself threatened. (ibid.: 55)

Why indeed would a shy animal, happiest when its dwelling is empty of people, come out in terror only when the synagogue is full? When this fragment is read in conjunction with the description of the Torah in the *Letter to His Father*, the animal as it faces the congregation seems to be the Torah itself. In the *Letter*, the adult Kafka reminisces that the moment when the Ark was opened "always reminded me of the shooting galleries where a cupboard door would open in the same way whenever one hit a bull's eye; except that there something interesting always came out and here it was always just the same old dolls without heads" (1976: 77). The terror of the animal becomes quite understandable if we picture it exposed as a target at a shooting gallery; the image of the Torah scrolls as headless dolls is doubled by the image of the animal's unwinking eyes, unable to see anything but the dangers by which it feels itself threatened. The terrified animal could also be

Kafka himself; he recalls being frightened "because of all the people one came into close contact with, but also because you once mentioned in passing that I too might be called to the Torah" (ibid.). Is it mere coincidence that, in the collection of Kafka's *Parables and Paradoxes*, "The Animal in the Synagogue" is immediately followed by the famous fragment "Before the Law?"

The child's terror at the prospect of being called upon to perform in public a ritual he utterly fails to understand need not be traced to any neurotic complex. The boredom Kafka remembers from the synagogue is familiar enough to me and to so many other Jewish children who were compelled to go by their parents' nostalgia for something that had once been alive — a furry, elusive animal perhaps. Kafka suggests, in sum, that his father's Judaism had come to be a frozen, defensive posture, not an autonomous ground of selfhood that could serve as an opening toward the Other.

What Kafka could not quite anticipate was just how much reason for defensiveness there was. The synagogues *are* granaries now, if they are still standing, not just in the little villages the Jews abandoned at the turn of the century, but in cities that had thousands of Jews during Kafka's lifetime. It is not the awareness of a life that has slipped away, even before the great catastrophe, that distinguishes Kafka here; the theme of disappearing worlds is prominent in Jewish writing since at least the nineteenth century (Kugelmass and Boyarin 1983). What makes the brief scene in the synagogue from the *Letter to His Father* and the fragment on "The Animal in the Synagogue" so powerfully evocative is not that they *restore* a lost world to our vision, but precisely that they remind us that we are not the first generation to find that loss is the heart of our connection.[11]

This dwelling in loss, rather than in a richly detailed space reconstituted through memory, is another term for what Deleuze and Guattari (1986) call "deterritorialization." This deterritorialization is not just limited to the sociological fact of migration,[12] not just the experience of being uprooted, but an overcoming of the fixation on the metaphor of roots. Their analysis suggests that Kafka, having shed any expectations either of organic identification as a Jew or of fitting with the non-Jewish German literary world, was freed to outline not just a "minor literature," as they call it, but more precisely a minor ethnography. Kafka's ethnography writes a people's experience in history without presuming to circumscribe that experience, without turning persons into exemplars of a reified culture. Refusing rigid identifications between tradition and place, treating space and time in the same phrase, he knows that a world can disappear in the village just when its echo is heard in Prague.

Kafka's writing of Jewishness contrasts most sharply with the rhetoric used by the convert Gottfried Selig, described earlier. Selig writes a comprehensive and distancing grammar of Yiddish from the perspective of a former insider; Kafka pretends to no expertise except the sense that there once must have been something rich and living. Selig employs frozen racial stereotypes to brand Yiddish as a "Hottentot" tongue; Kafka turns animals into sacred texts and sacred texts into dolls, enhancing the Otherness of the tradition without romanticizing its place in his own history. Selig likens the rejected Other within to the fantasized Other without, attempting to reterritorialize himself in a newly bounded time and space; Kafka chips away at the same boundaries without pretending that they do not exist. Kafka's minor ethnography suggests that we look more closely at the silencing of Europe's Jewish other within. We may gain some desperately needed clues concerning the way that ominously self-identical continent managed for so long to contain the threat of the colonial Other without, and indeed, concerning the way the ultimate violent removal of the first from Europe is linked to Europe's loss of control of the second.

Six

The Impossible International

and there is room for all at the
convocation of conquest
Aimè Césaire (1983: 77)

Isaac Babel, a Jew from Odessa, wrote his collection of stories called *Red Cavalry* on the basis of the time he spent attached to a Bolshevik Cossack unit fighting in the Russo–Polish war just after the First World War.[1] Many of the stories revolve around the conflict inside the author among the nostalgic pull of Jewish identity, the ringing principles of revolution, and the violent virility of the Cossacks. The sketch called "Gedali," describing the narrator's meeting with an elderly Jewish storekeeper in the city of Zhitomir, is one of the most powerful. It begins with a paragraph that could have been written by a hundred Jewish writers at the turn of the century:

> On Sabbath eves I am oppressed by the dense melancholy of
> memories. In bygone days on these occasions my grandfather
> would stroke the volumes of Ibn Ezra with his yellow beard.
> His old woman in her lace cap would trace fortunes with her
> knotty fingers over the Sabbath candles, and sob softly to
> herself. On those evenings my child's heart was rocked like
> a little ship upon enchanted waves. O the rotted Talmuds of
> my childhood! O the dense melancholy of memories! (Babel
> 1955: 69)

The narrator then describes one such Sabbath eve's melancholy, which brings him into Gedali's "old curiosity shop." A dialogue between the

99

two men ensues. Despite the young writer's stout insistence that the International "is eaten with gunpowder . . . and spiced with best-quality blood," Gedali clearly holds the moral upper ground: "And here we are, all of us learned people, falling on our faces and crying out in a loud voice: 'Woe unto us, where is the joy-giving Revolution?' " The dialogue ends as night falls. The old man departs; "Gedali, the founder of an impossible International, has gone to the synagogue to pray."

This little scene highlights resonant questions about the links between intimate memory and the politics of world-transforming revolution. The writer, cast on the waves of history without a ship to rock in, goes looking for the parents of his parent, trying to satisfy his melancholy memories of a fragile peace doomed to extinction. He is able to make contact with someone like his grandfather, through the link of a shared Jewishness, but it is impossible to sustain that link; he will not surrender his vision of the necessary violence of the Revolution, and Gedali will not surrender his Sabbath. Gedali's phrase, "all of us learned people," harks back to the text of the Passover Haggadah, a tale of ancient Jewish liberation, only to sharpen the illusory character of *this* revolution's claims for liberation. An "International" that is imposed on subject nations—since that was the Bolshevik goal in the invasion of Poland—is no international at all, yet the dream of a truly international, joy-giving revolution is an impossible one.

If Babel restricted himself to this portrait of an "impossible" encounter without trying to make programmatic political capital out of it, how can we dare to take up and use this fragile sketch now, when all the rotting Talmuds of Eastern Europe are gone, along with all the skeptical hopes generated by the Bolshevik Revolution? What can I do with this immobilized memory of the dream of an impossible International? The worst thing would be to use the wisdom of Gedali to enshrine once again the memory of East European Jews within some imaginary Holocaust museum. That would seal the deaths of Gedali and of Babel (killed by Stalin) once again. The way to make the memory live is to begin to ask how the impossible International might look today.

"Gedali" is one of an infinite number of specific starting points, all of which are indispensable and "unforgettable" (see chapter 1, n. 2). It is powerful because of the worlds it brings together, not because Jews are altogether unique as a people of memory (see chapter 5). Similar questions about how to articulate intimate memories with current co-alition politics arise in other collective traditions, as in bell hooks's meditations on her African-American Southern grandmother's history quilts (hooks 1990).[2] To evoke Jewish history as it was lived on the eve of the great destruction should not only set that history apart, but also bring it within the purview of a growing dialogue about the politics of memory and the mutuality of difference. This cannot be done by a resuscitation of the past that attempts to sneak around the gulf of the Nazi genocide. Rather, one task, if we mean to dream once again about Gedali's "impossible International," is to work against the idea that "the Jewish question" is no longer on the political agenda of the right *or* the left. Overcoming this silencing of discourse on the po-litical role of Jewish difference requires of critical discourse both that it consider how anti-Semitism was integrated with the range of Fascist repressions and that it recognizes that the problematics of modernity that contributed to the Nazi taking of power were not solved as a re-sult of the Allied victory.

The silencing of discourse about Jewish difference is generally ac-complished through the subsumption of Jews within categories pre-sumed to be dominant. Two examples are available in a recent issue of the journal *Cultural Critique*. There, Nancy Hartsock refers in passing to the "dominant white, male, Eurocentric ruling class" (1987: 192); and Henry Louis Gates argues the need to get "away from a Eurocen-tric notion of a hierarchical 'canon' of texts, mostly white, Western and male. " (1987: 31-32). Such examples can be multiplied. Now, I grant that some shorthand is inevitable, some ways of categorizing the dominators and the dominated, in order to speak critically about col-lective subjects at all. Yet it is curious that the term *Christian* almost never figures on such lists. The identification of the elite by "objec-tive" characteristics including geographic location, gender, and skin color obscures the way that specific, often local, histories effect con-tingent hierarchies of privilege and exclusion. There is likewise some-thing Eurocentric in the implicit assumption that these hierarchies and distinctions are as generously inclusive of all culture produced within Europe (such as Yiddish culture) as they are exclusive of that produced outside Europe.[3]

To a degree, such shortfalls in critical conceptualization may be traced to the syndrome by which many theorists are silent about the connection between their Jewishness and their critique, or worse, perpetuate myths about the Jewish origins of various forms of ideological domination. A spectacular example is that of Hélène Cixous. At the beginning of her essay "Sorties," she lays out her Outsider credentials as colonized, Jew, woman, and honorary Arab:

> Me, too. The routine "our ancestors, the Gauls" was pulled on me. But I was born in Algeria, and my ancestors lived in Spain, Morocco, Austria, Hungary, Czechoslovakia, Germany; my brothers by birth are Arab. So where are we in history? I side with those who are injured, trespassed upon, civilized. I am (not) Arab. Who am I? I am "doing" French history. I am a Jewish woman. (1986: 71)

The initial move here is promising: against the fetishization of Gallic ethnoterritorialism, Cixous insists on a deterritorialized genealogy of memory. Yet once she has established her credentials in this fashion, her biography drops away. She opts for a politics of solidarity, bravely volunteering whose "side" she is on. She avoids consideration of the ambiguous situation of North African Jews, so frequently "in between" the French colonizers and the Muslim colonized, who are described by Albert Memmi as trying

> to resemble the colonizer in the frank hope that he may cease to consider them different from him. . . . But if the colonizer does not always openly discourage these candidates to develop that resemblance, he never permits them to attain it either. Thus, they live in painful and constant ambiguity. (1967: 15)

Cixous is not really interested in tracing out the strands of her identity, in formulating an answer to the rhetorical "Who am I?" She speaks only, in declarative sentences, as Woman. The references to her Jewishness are all negative, and quickly fade away with the other specifics. The cost is considerable, not only because the experience of Jews in the French colonies destabilizes the artificial dichotomy between the world of the colonizer and the world of the colonized,[4] but also because she goes on carelessly to blame Jewish tradition for much of her oppression as a woman. She refers casually to "biblicocapitalist" society (95) after explaining that "I have not read the Bible" (73). While taking pains to criticize Freud's fantasy of penis envy, she confidently refers to Freud's bizarre text *Moses and Monotheism*[5] in a section headed "the dawn of phallocentrism" (100–102). She cites Freud's claim that a historical turn away from maternity toward paternity, and Moses' positing of an invisible God, are both victories "of spirituality over the senses." Then, under the appropriative caption "Jewoman," she links this to Kafka's parable about the man from the country waiting vainly all his life to be admitted to the Law. The Law and God are only this repressive fiction. The figure of the Jew is only interesting to Cixous here as the victim of the Mosaic law that the Jew is responsible for anyway: "It 'is' hence it is only if he makes it." Having served his purpose, the Jew becomes woman, and the discussion moves to Greek mythology, which is what really moves Cixous.

Pointing these patterns out is worthwhile in itself. But it is also intended to help clarify my main point. I would like to begin to articulate a claim that the collective security of Jews and the search for Jewish communication entail important common interests with feminism and anti-imperialism. Fundamental to this claim is our understanding of Nazism, something to which both the anticolonialist and the feminist critiques of the still-dominant mode of knowledge can make vital contributions. The articulation among Jewish concerns and the concerns of other threatened collective subjects was never as clear as it needed to be and is virtually extinct at present. The absence of that articulation is, I believe, material to the maintenance of several dimensions of hierarchy. Furthermore, the dangers posed by this failure are not only theoretical, and not only to Jews. Thus, for example, Gates uncritically reiterates Wole Soyinka's description of apartheid as "the last, institutionally functioning product of archaic articles of Euro-Judaic thought" (1987: 45). Unless Gates and Soyinka take the trouble to explain this phrase, I am left with two conclusions. One is that they confuse a particular form of anti-Jewish rhetoric—the claim that the ancient Hebrews invented and then disseminated the poison of ethnic chauvinism—with a critique of Eurocentrism. The other is that they attribute injustice to the persistence of archaic ideas—a curious stance for those who would criticize the prejudices of the "Western" Enlightenment.[6]

I would not want thinkers and writers such as Gates and Soyinka to stop commenting on Jewish issues, however. On the contrary. The fact that there seem to be so many Jewish scholars of black studies and African studies, and so few African-American or African scholars of Jewish studies, indicates a relative luxury enjoyed by Jews. Yet it is a "luxury" for which Jews and Jewish scholarship pay dearly. Jews will only be in a safe and healthy position when our self-image can be challenged and enriched by an informed critique from a variety of others. No one owes us this critique, of course, nor is it really possible except within the context of much broader social changes. Yet the parochial isolation of Jewish thought is inseparable from a situation in which most self-identified Jews understand their collective security needs in ways that strike the rest of the world as narrow-mindedly exclusive. Failing a sustained contentious dialogue with a variety of collective others, even without an immediate threat to our physical well-being, Jews leave ourselves in the vulnerable position of having no authoritative collective stance except the paranoid fanaticism of Itzhak Shamir and his ilk.

My argument, therefore, is not simply that we must speak in our own Jewish voice and that we must speak to others as well. The larger point is that voices speaking with various Jewish accents, with a range of Jewish associations, have to be interlocutors in a global discussion of our common fate. The agenda, for Jews, is largely set by the demands of an impossible balancing act between the anamnestic claims of past Jewish generations and the universalist claims of present humanity, since what Judaism has to contribute to the global discussion stems largely from an ancient notion of partial and shared human responsibility for redemption. More urgently and precisely, the critical attempt to link the enormity of Jewish suffering at midcentury with global perspectives on oppression and liberation calls for some way to characterize our contemporaneity, "our time." Such a characterization cannot rely on progressivist notions of gradual emancipation from "archaic articles of thought." Nor can it afford to dismiss the past decades as the time when hope yielded to despair, growing unity to chaotic atomization.

Instead, this problem draws me to Julia Kristeva's sentence about "[our] time . . . that seems to have, for a century now, gone into unending labor pains" (1982: 23). What should we say about this epigraph? Or, as one of my classmates said, "It's a beautiful image—but what makes it specific to the twentieth century?" Why privilege linear, calendrical delineations when demarcating historical periods? What is it that our century is trying to give birth to, and why mystify the agonizing pain of childbirth by speaking as if it could be accomplished by "a century"?

Part of our century's "labor pains," many would agree, can also be described as the death throes of a certain form of modernism. Sometimes the resulting situation is lampooned: postmodernism is dismissed as postmortem. But the best of postmodern theorizing does not stop at demystification, decentering, deconstruction. It begins to explore how the world can be known from a multiplicity of enunciated centers. This positive moment in postmodernism is inseparable from political engagement. As Nancy Hartsock asks, in the article I criticized earlier, "the most pressing question for those of us [cultural theorists] committed to social change is what we can replace modernism with" (1987: 204).

Answers to this "pressing question" will not come from theory separated from history. I believe there is something of epochal difference marking our history since 1914. In trying to identify that difference, I provisionally view the period from 1914 through 1945 as the extended duration of world war, and then identify the postmodern period as beginning at the end of World War II. An attempt to define the specificity of our century (inadequate as it still must be) may bring us a bit closer toward understanding the interrelated problematics of movements such as Third World liberationism, feminism, and the struggle to reinvent Jewishness.

I suggest that what is distinctive about our "postmodern" time is, to a decisive degree, the fact of living after two paroxysms of imperialism turned inward, especially Nazism and Fascism. Both World Wars may be regarded as symptoms of imperialism having reached its limits. One of the causes of the first, as historians seem to agree, was Germany's frustration at having entered the race for the world so late that there was little territory outside Europe to conquer. Furthermore, Aimè Césaire argued powerfully that one source of the genocidal obsession of the second was the experience of dehumanization acquired in the course of the colonial encounter. He wrote in his *Discourse on Colonialism*:

First we must study how colonization works to *decivilize* the

colonizer, to *brutalize* him in the true sense of the word, to
degrade him, to awaken him to buried instincts, to
covetousness, violence, race hatred, and moral relativism; and
we must show that each time a head is cut off or an eye put
out in Vietnam and in France they accept the fact, each time
a Madagascan is tortured and in France they accept the fact,
civilization acquires another dead weight, a universal
regression takes place, a gangrene sets in, a center of infection
begins to spread; and that at the end of all these treaties that
have been violated, all these lies that have been propagated,
all these punitive expeditions that have been tolerated, all
these prisoners who have been tied up and "interrogated," all
these patriots who have been tortured, at the end of all the
racial pride that has been encouraged, all the boastfulness that
has been displayed, a poison has been instilled into the veins
of Europe and, slowly but surely, the continent proceeds
toward *savagery*.

Yes, it would be worthwhile to study clinically, in detail,
the steps taken by Hitler and Hitlerism and to reveal to the
very distinguished, very humanistic, very Christian bourgeois
of the twentieth century that without his being aware of it, he
has a Hitler inside him, that Hitler *inhabits* him, that Hitler is
his *demon*, that if he rails against him, he is being inconsistent
and that, at bottom, it is not *the humiliation of man as such*,
it is the crime against the white man, the humiliation of the
white man, and the fact that he applied to Europe colonialist
procedures which until then had been reserved exclusively for
the Arabs of Algeria, the coolies of India, and the blacks of
Africa. (1972: 13–14)

The long quote from Césaire is necessary mostly because of its passionate truth. Note well that the reference to Hitler's "crime against
the white man" does not itself obscure the focus on eliminating Jews:
what Césaire is mocking is the bourgeois Christian European's fantasy
that he had brought the Jew *as* "white man" under the protective umbrella of civilization, safe from the colonial storm. But beyond this insight, it is also important for me, as a Jew, to repeat those names
Madagascar, Vietnam . . . and to add the name Jew, since brutality inside
the metropole as well as outside prepared the way for genocide . . .

and to add the name Palestine, since the victims are often brutal-
ized in turn, and since we must always do what we can, now.

The genocide at the heart of the second war, then, must not be divorced from the imperial causes of the first. And our present situation
is linked to the outcome of that second war. The doubt about progress
that characterizes postmodernism, the frequent conviction that our
energies and conceptions are inadequate to the task of complete liberation, are related to the ambiguous victories (and the generally unac-
knowledged ambiguous moral position) of the Allied forces. Thus
Lyotard, referring to the Second World War as "a kind of civil war,"
explains that there could be no unambiguous and satisfactory judgment at Nuremberg "because the constitution of the Nuremburg tri-
bunal required an Allied victory . . . the criminal was able to see in his
judge merely a criminal more fortunate than he in the conflict of
arms" (1988: 56).[7]

The results of the extended world war were not a defeat of imperialism per se, as the postwar language of spheres of influence and the
Pax Americana showed. Furthermore, the effort to pin the genocidal
impulse on the German national character quickly proved hollow.
Postwar thought is haunted by the inadequacy of modern ideologies
such as liberalism and positive Marxism and informed by the lesson
that Western Enlightenment is inseparable from Western imperialism,
but intellectuals from the former Allied countries (and how much
more so, God help them, German intellectuals) are struggling to learn
how to think Otherwise. No wonder the doctrine of the divided subject is popular.

And yet, just as clearly, imperialism isn't what it was, and another
factor of postmodern questioning of progress stems from the weak-
ened partnership of Enlightenment and imperialism. That partnership
does not dissolve of itself. Its exposure is the result both of immediate
political struggle and of engaged critiques like those of Césaire, Gates,
Soyinka, and Hartsock. It is not too much to say that I owe the life I
have made for myself as a Jew in large measure to such critiques. Were
I less equipped by them to criticize Enlightenment assumptions—were
I limited to the Enlightenment's own terms—my choices would likewise have been restricted. I could have limited myself to the nineteenth-century German Jewish style of detached academic study
known as *Wissenschaft des Judentums*—the science of Judaism (note the

possessive form). Or I could have restricted myself to immersion in Jewish text and law, abandoning "the dream of a common language" (Rich 1978). Either choice would have left me half alive.

And so I turned in two directions: toward Yiddish, in order to understand more about Gedali's world; and toward critical theory, in order to learn how to transform nostalgia into critical power. Thus a critical text for me in coming to understand the link between Enlightenment and imperialism was Horkheimer and Adorno's *Dialectic of Enlightenment*. Victimization by Nazism led these two men—German Jews hardly disposed to theorize on the basis of autobiography—to ask how the liberating project of Enlightenment could lead to Fascism. Their answer (the point seems almost obvious now, but partly because of the critique they produced forty years ago) was that there is an equation between the fiction of universal, abstract reason and the fiction of universal, abstract value (money), both of which are mystified tools of Christian European world dominance. Their ideas are germaine to the discourse on the politics of difference at the end of the twentieth century:

> In magic there is specific representation. . . . In science. . . . [r]epresentation is exchanged for the fungible—universal interchangeability. . . . Enlightenment dissolves the injustice of the old inequality—unmediated lordship and mastery—but at the same time perpetuates it in universal mediation, in the relation of any one existent to the other . . . it excises the incommensurable. . . . The universality of ideas is developed by discursive logic, domination in the conceptual sphere is raised up on the basis of actual domination. . . .
> Enlightenment is mythic fear turned radical. . . . Nothing at all may remain outside, because the mere idea of outsidedness is the very source of fear. (1972: 10, 12, 14, 16)

The relevant point can be made more explicit. Césaire takes colonialism as a starting point and portrays Nazi brutality as colonial practices brought home. Horkheimer and Adorno work outward from the Enlightenment inside Europe, suggesting that the claim that everything on the globe can be rationally known contributes to the drive to control everything on the globe. Horkheimer and Adorno teach us to beware of Césaire's implication that, prior to the brutalization undergone by the colonizer in the process of domination, the reality of European liberal civilization approached its own ideal. Césaire reminds us that the colonies were the school where dominant Europeans learned how to de-differentiate masses of people and transform them into fungible commodities.

Horkheimer and Adorno came close to enunciating their own interested difference in the last chapter of *Dialectic of Enlightenment*. In that chapter, "Elements of Anti-Semitism," they note that "from the outset there has always been an intimate link between anti-Semitism and totality" (ibid: 172). And yet, despite the pathos of their histories as victims of anti-Semitism, Horkheimer and Adorno retained a paradoxically objective, authoritative, "Enlightened" tone in this book. They did not present themselves as victims or as actors—perhaps because they were unaware of the particular origins in Christian European history of the distanced stance their critique reproduces.[8]

This revealing lapse may be related to another, which is glaringly obvious to a contemporary reader: Horkheimer and Adorno failed to anticipate the insight that authoritarian universalist reason is a specifically male fiction (G. Lloyd 1985; Irigaray 1985). Perhaps, in fact, their arguments seem impossibly outdated to some because the postmodern debate about the knowing subject is in fact most acutely articulated in feminist theory, where the interrogation of the concept of identity is paradoxically but vitally dependent upon the assertion of a contestatory identity. Thus Hartsock cuts to the "center" of this issue by locating it within the liberation project.

> The "center" will obviously look different when occupied by women and men of color and white women than it does now, when occupied by white men of a certain class background. Indeed, given our diversity, it may cease to look like a center at all. But, as for being peripheral, we've done that for far too long. (1987: 204)

But here's the rub: this statement provides a short list of privileged "Othereds" (women and people of color) who are now to get a chance at the center. This is one problem with what constitutes, in effect, a rhetoric of coalition. Some on the margins are still absent from the catalogue of those who are to be brought to the center.[9]

Another problem with such coalition rhetoric is that it focuses on the analogies among various minorities only insofar as they are oppressed and therefore, presumably, "progressively" inclined. This is the oppositionalist counterpart of the liberal version of pluralism, in which the differences among, for example, African-Americans, Irish-Americans, and Jewish Americans are merely the spice of life. Such politics of analogy tend to mask the material and cultural conflicts that are part of the reason why these groups remain distinct. Hartsock's rhetoric also freezes the identities of people "of color" and "white women"; it elides the way those identities vary, notably between center and margin. Thus I need to say that in fixing on this brief quote, I am not saying that Jews, too, aren't at the center and should be. In *some* situations it is indeed easier for (especially male) Jews to "pass" and thus approach the centers of power. But they generally get to the center only at the cost of vitiating any liberatory force their Jewishness might offer. Sometimes at least, for Jews as for others, the approach to the center is compelled: "the so-called non-West's turn toward the West is a command" (Spivak 1990: 8). The blind spots—and not just the stunning insights—in Horkheimer and Adorno's German neo-Marxist critical theory could well be related to a link between their authoritative male stance and a discursively enforced silencing of their histories as German Jews.

There are sufficient reasons then to be wary of analogizing, rather than articulating, different centers of marginality. This is perhaps especially true of those names, such as "woman" and "Jew," that are sometimes employed as master tropes of oppression. Catherine MacKinnon juxtaposes precisely these two names, in furtherance of her discussion of the specificity of women's oppression and her claim that "the woman question" should be "seen as *the* question, calling for analysis in its own terms" (1982: 527).

> If I say, "Such and such is true for women," and someone
> responds, "But it's not the same for all women," that is
> supposed to undercut the statement rather than point out
> features that comprise the sex-specificity of the thing. [But]
> . . . all it proves to say that something is not the same for all
> women is that it is not biological, not that it is not gendered.
> . . . That some non-Jews, such as gypsys and gays, were
> victims of the Holocaust does not mean the Holocaust was

not, or was less, anti-Semitic. . . . We . . . know something about the *content* of the Holocaust, I trust, that makes it impossible to present isolated if significant counterexamples as if they undercut the specific meaning of the atrocities for the groups who were *defined* by their subjection to them. (1988: 111-12)

MacKinnon's sensitivity to the memory and experience of Jews (and which other "groups"?) is worth emphasizing. More interesting to me, however, is that in effect she uses Jews as a *subordinate term* in an analogy to women's oppression, and she fails to think the term through. That Nazi atrocities have "a specific [defining] meaning" for some groups of victims does not in any way entail the further assertion that other groups are "isolated counterexamples." What are they isolated from, what were they counterexamples to, and how could that possibly affect the memory of those (e.g., gypsys and gays) who mourn them? In order to preserve the autonomous Jewish experience of Nazism in support of her analogy, she separates Jews from other victims of the Nazis. She thus risks acceding to the mythified uniqueness of the Jewish genocide, à la Elie Wiesel and the President's Holocaust Commission. This image of "uniqueness" is certainly tied to the fact that the Final Solution evolved into a precedent for concentrated, obsessive, high-tech genocide. But insofar as the Holocaust is granted a privileged place of horror because it happened *inside the center of empire* (as Césaire pointed out), the isolation of Jewish oppression is a key ideology-effect of neoimperialism. By occluding the tie between anti-Semitism and imperialism, it blocks linkage between the interests of Jews and of others living within a post-genocidal, postcolonial situation. Moreover, the implication that the real "definition" of Jews is through their subjection to genocide precludes the possibility of an internally differentiated contemporary Jewish collective with a range of autonomous linkages with non-Jews. Placing Jewish experience in a box labeled "the Holocaust" and privileging it as a special suffering confined to the Nazi years reinforces the illusion that the state of emergency under Fascism was the exception rather than the rule (see Benjamin 1969b).[10] In order to see the political nature of continued, autonomous Jewish existence at the end of the twentieth century, faced with the horrors that continue to define our world, it is important to disrupt the definition of Jews solely by the suffering of the Holocaust, to distinguish, that is, "between [a critical] intervention which radically discriminates between broadly defined cultural practices and military atrocities and one that insists on the continuity—the seamless, however differential, relationship—between them" (Spanos 1990: 220).

Again, this is not to gainsay MacKinnon's point—which I appreciate her having made—about the specificity of Nazi anti-Semitism. But that insight needs to be linked to a call to explore the historical logic of the *range* of oppressions Nazism entails. MacKinnon's analogy stands meanwhile as a promising challenge to theory. Feminism represents the possibility of a solidarity that can account for differences and still be so broadly and materially based as to approach the "universal" without mystification. Hence feminist theory contains—more than any other body of theory—the tools for an account of Nazi ideology and practice explaining, on the one hand, the connections among the oppression of Jews, other "inferior" races, radicals, "sexual deviants," the handicapped[11]—and on the other hand the existence of a Nazi women's sphere that served to "humanize" the Third Reich by defining the "safe" realm of the Nazi state's inside. Such an account might look back to the scholarship of nineteenth-century West European nationalism, which among its other achievements detected a systematic distinction between the feminine, inert, and passive Semites and the masculine, creative, and mobile Aryans (Olender 1989: 147 ff.). It could continue by interrogating the connections between the military drive for conquest of *Lebensraum* and that other *Lebensraum* that, to Nazi women, "meant a peaceful social sphere within which women of all classes and ages would cooperate to revive the gospel of love and harmony" (Koonz 1987: 13). It would then search for articulations among capitalist greed for exploitable labor, patriarchal obsessions with camaraderie and female purity (Theweleit 1987, 1989), racist paranoia about "degeneration" (see, e.g., Mosse 1985), and the Nazi fantasy of self-generation through "the creative power of myth in general" (Lacoue-Labarthe and Nancy 1989: 307). Finally, given the explicit linkage in feminist theory between historical considerations and problems of the present, it would seek to substantiate, and not merely reiterate, hypotheses about the link between Nazi oppression and liberal repression.[12]

Similarly, I suggest, critical feminist perspectives have a place in all attempts to understand the sources and (mis)uses of authority and knowledge. Theory, including feminist theory, can be described as the work of finding or creating language to articulate in dialogue (sometimes in adversarial dialogue—cf. Esonwanne 1990-91) the relations among various and shifting identities, memories and situations. The interrogation of the collective name—woman, Jew, and many others—without dismantling the possibility of speaking it is one of the most general contributions of feminist theory.

At last I can suggest an answer to the question of what it is to which our century is trying to give birth. Admittedly that answer is laughably grandiose. But don't we need to be able to talk about grandiose things and laugh about them at the same time? Our century has witnessed the limits of imperialist expansion, the achievement of a world system in which we cannot save ourselves alone, only each other, together. The era we are entering is the time when we will liberate ourselves collectively or extinguish ourselves collectively.[13]

The Great War that began in 1914 became, in retrospect, the First World War, the beginning of the war for the world, a war none of the combatants could fully win or lose. The turning point those decades mark is, however, in the history of imperialism the point at which the strictly geographical demarcations between the colonialist world and the colonized world break down. The colonized occupy the metropole as *Gastarbeiter* (guest workers) who sometimes overstay their welcome, occupy the metropole, and the ideology of the unified, monocultural nation-state begins gradually to crack.

The effects of this ideological questioning are echoed, it seems to me, in the history of feminism. In France, for example, Naomi Schor (1989) has analyzed the progression from what she calls de Beauvoir's critique of "othering"—a critique mounted in the name of women's equality against the image of a female essence that makes the home the appropriate sphere for women—to Luce Irigaray's critique of "saming," a critique mounted in an effort to construct a "fluid" feminine alternative to male, monolithic, imperious subjectivity. The difference between de Beauvoir's insistence that women be admitted into the dominant French intellectual class and Irigaray's attempt to deconstruct Western intellectualism in general from the standpoint of woman has to do with the slippage between a time when the French monocultural ideal (Paris, the capital of the nineteenth century) still held and a time when that image was rapidly giving way to recognition of a plural French society, in which the population of the former colonies enters the metropolis.[14]

In France, the defense of pluralism (however agonistic and incommensurate) meets today with resistance in the form of Le Pen's neo-Fascist movement. It is ironic but in a bizarre way fitting that the rhetoric of Le Pen—one-time defender of "l'Algérie française"—exploits the myth of a "pure" France (the France of the Maid of Orleans) besieged and invaded by the barbarian hordes of the formerly colonized! The Le Pen phenomenon is both ominous and actually life-killing every day it exists, and yet . . . the terms have changed. The presence of millions of North and West Africans and other immigrants in France, whatever the unequal dynamics of power that result in their presence there, is breaking down the ideological link between coterritoriality and cultural identity. The immigrants are breaking down the geographical categorization of persons. The world is coming to the seat of empire; there is room for everyone at the convocation of conquest.

Room for the Jews as well? Yes. What is "Jewish" happens to be mine. But it is also a critical term in the web of the postimperial world. Its continued importance may be surprising, since it usually seems as though the "Jewish question" had been obviated by genocide, by the ideological reduction of difference in liberalism,[15] and by the collapse of the Soviet empire. Showing that the question is still with us requires a realization, available in feminist theories and discussions of postcoloniality, that the human subject is simultaneously culturally constructed and historically embodied.[16] Critical reflection on Jewish experience can offer important caveats to theory—such as Emmanuel Lévinas's warning that dissatisfaction with the Enlightenment disembodiment of subjectivity has *also* led to Nazi territorial--organicist racism (1990; cf. Kaplan 1989, especially 161). This work of theoretically articulating so many alternative traditions, so many dimensions of exclusion, requires the utmost attention to the experience of suffering. It must also draw on the resources of autonomous invention, perhaps the most important of which is memory, which offers the possibility of a play of difference transcending the seeming alternatives of hierarchy and of leveling. The work is constricted in different ways by the fiction of unsituated objectivity and by the tone of aggrieved or triumphalist solidarity, yet it can completely escape neither. To veer toward the former by way of conclusion, I would state that theory at its most vital interrogates histories and identities in ways that avoid rhetorically displacing one oppression or identity onto another; presume a shared human interest, while resisting the urges to define and reify "it" or prescribe a singular method for achieving "it"; and press unremittingly for equitable distribution of access to discourse.

Seven

Palestine and Jewish History

November 1989

The title of this chapter refers to two distinct and interrelated denotations of the term *Palestine*. The first designates that region between Lebanon, the Sinai, the Mediterranean, and the Jordan, particularly as it became a focus of activist Jewish collective aspirations in the modern period. The second is the name of a new state, declared at the meeting of the Palestine National Council in Algiers in November 1988, intended to be the national home of the Palestinian Arab people. My intention in this chapter, then, is to interrogate the consequences of the first Palestine having become the prime grounding of Jewish collective identity since World War II and, more immediately, to interrogate the challenge to that grounding presented by the second Palestine and by its popular manifestation, the *intifada*. I understand the *intifada* as a challenge not only to "Zionist ideology and propaganda" but also more generally to Western conceptions of state, territory, and nation—in the long run, to the idea that state power can be a satisfactory repository and guarantor of collective identity.

Before World War II, the same word, *Palestine*, that quickens the hearts of Palestinian Arabs around the world today had the same effect on many Jewish youth in Eastern Europe and elsewhere. Some of the descendants of those Jewish youth are now Israelis actively denying the existence and the rights of the new Palestine. For them, it is the term that has changed over time, not the referent. What was Palestine for their grandparents is now *Eretz Yisrael Hashleyma*—Greater Israel. The limits of the Palestinian state, however, are not the same as those of the historical region of Palestine. In Israeli consciousness, then, Palestine is obsolete; it has been superseded. In current Palestinian politics, Palestine has been restricted to those areas outside the pre-1967 borders of Israel and therefore excludes the center of historical Palestine. Thus Palestine is and is not Palestine. Geography is not determinate and fixed, but is an object of social construction and contention. To a large extent, geography is a product of and a resource in the struggle of groups of people to attain legitimacy and power simultaneously—that is, to make and establish themselves as nations.

Literate Westerners (on the level of shared discourse represented, for example, by the *New York Times*) commonly suppose that the process of state formation is a complementary one—that when new states are declared and established, they are welcomed and integrated into the so-called community of nations. In this case, however, the positing of the Palestinian Arab state appears to challenge the premises of another, existing state—the Jewish state of Israel.

The challenge may be stated thus: How is one collective, which may be variously labeled Zionists, Jews, or Israelis for different purposes, justified in maintaining or renewing its collective identity at the expense of the collective identity and practical well-being of another, the Palestinians? The answer that there was no other choice is insufficient. Rather the answer is that Jewish experience in the twentieth century (not just the experience of genocide) itself challenges the modern European conception of the proper organization of polities.

I am moved to articulate these challenges, as a committed Jew, largely as a result of a published debate between my brother and me, on the one hand, and Edward Said, on the other (Said 1989d; Boyarin and Boyarin 1989). In the course of his rejoinder, Professor Said complained that our discussions of the Jewish historical context of Zionism and the Palestinians should not be addressed to Palestinians, but rather to our fellow Jews. Though I still see no reason why the *intifada* obviates dialogue between Jewish and Palestinian intellectuals about subjects including Jewish history, I want to take his challenge seriously. The lessons the *intifada* teaches about Jewish history are in the first instance lessons for Jews, not lessons to Palestinians. I want, therefore, precisely to take the *intifada* as an opportunity to question

the strategy—hegemonic in post–World War II Jewish discourse—of
grounding Jewish identity primarily in a territory "we" control (not,
for most Jews, even a space "we" live in!), rather than in our nuanced
collective memory.

It seems almost gratuitous to state that my point is not to dismantle
the state of Israel. But if the Israeli state, once established, is implicitly
understood by its own elites as a *static* reality dependent on functional
equilibrium, then a threat to any of its parts (including its self-gener-
ated history) is a threat to its very existence. Related to the equilibrium
model is the image of the nation as an integral collective. If the nation
is seen as a "body," an organism, then to take apart and examine its
history is to stop its heart from beating. This may make it easier to
understand why the *intifada*'s challenge is being resisted so relentlessly—as if the galvanized Palestinians were a dangerous virus. It
certainly explains why it is practically and not merely theoretically urgent for those interested in the welfare of *both* groups to insist that the
state is neither static nor a body.

The European nationalist worldview in which that static, organicist
conception of Israeli nationhood is based is sharply outlined by the
Israeli scholar Juval Portugali in an essay on "Nationalism, Social
Theory, and the Israeli/Palestinian Case." The critical point for this
discussion is his explanation of "the generative social order," based on
earlier theoretical work by David Bohm and H. Haken:

> Holistic conceptions . . . start from the postulation that there
> is movement and disequilibrium and consequently what must
> be explained is how stability is created and terminated. Here
> entities are seen as spatially and temporally confined formal
> appearances, or events.
>
> Stability is achieved when a given configuration of events
> predominate. The amplitude of this configuration is termed
> "generative order" [or] "order parameter". . . . Once a given
> order parameter is established, other events or configurations
> "are subjected to the newly established order state or, they are
> 'enslaved' by the order parameter". . . . [N]ationalism became
> the generative order in modern society, first, in the sense that
> world society was, and still is, "forced" to organize according
> to its order principles and, second, in the sense that other
> major social orders, such as capitalism and communism,

accept (i.e. were enslaved by) its principles. (Portugali 1988: 154)

An example of how compelling this generative order still can be is found in a recent enthusiastic description of the *intifada* by Edward Said:

> Above all the sense that the *intifada* demonstrated a collectivity or community finding its way together is what was most impressive. The source of this is the organic nationhood that today underlies Palestinian life. For the first time Palestinians exposed themselves to it, allowed themselves to be guided by it directly, offered themselves to its imperatives. Instead of individuals and private interests, the public good and the collective will predominated. Leaders were never identified. Personalities were submerged in the group. (1989a: 37)

Two points in this statement stand out in light of Portugali's analysis: first that, as during the *intifada*, people do seem to be galvanized by national sentiment toward selfless, altruistic organization and sacrifice at certain moments in their history; and second, that even as perspicacious a secular critic as Said can become caught up in the rhetoric of "organic nationhood" that he would certainly abhor in Zionist, let alone direct European great power imperialist, contexts.

There is another essential aspect of the "generative social order" of nationalism that Portugali does not address. This is the notion that the path to peace and universal harmony lies in getting each national group properly *placed*, in the place where it belongs. Long before the twentieth century, the Jews were explicitly seen as an obstacle to this goal. According to Karl Morrison's recent book on empathy in Western thought, for the German philosopher Fichte at the end of the eighteenth century, there was "only one way in which the tension between dominant orders and the Jewish 'state within a state' could end and the Jewish obstacle to human unity be overcome—namely, the conquest of a homeland for the Jews and the deportation of them all to it" (Morrison 1988: xii). If, however, there is no place for the Jews, then within this nationalist framework the question becomes, as the title of a French essay puts it, whether we are "Un peuple de trop sur la terre" (Rabi 1979)—one too many nations for the world to support.

Within that framework, again, let me summarily rehearse the main arguments in favor of Zionist Jewish nationalism.

Vis-à-vis the rest of the world, Zionist and official Israeli ideology makes several claims:

a. Zionism would settle "homeless" people on an undeveloped land without a significant population;
b. it would introduce the benefits of civilization in a backward region; and
c. by creating the conditions for the reunification and regeneration of the Jewish nation, it would contribute to world order in general.

Vis-à-vis the set of all Jews, Zionism promised:

a. to provide a safe haven against persecution and guarantee Jews physical security;
b. to end the unnatural situation in which Jews were always located culturally and economically as a middleman minority by establishing an autonomous Jewish economy and thus assuring material security for people often excluded from developing industrial and professional spheres;
c. to regenerate Jews culturally by freeing them from a perpetual condition of marginal adherence to whatever cultures they lived among and renewing the powerful, vital, and integral ancient Hebrew language;
d. to regenerate Jews physically and morally through the creation of a society based on noncompetitive agricultural production and love of the earth; and
e. to put an end to centuries of wandering by returning Jews to their own historical homeland.

By creating the social conditions for a revival of the Hebrew language, Israel has indeed provided writers, scholars, and other creative workers with a new means to Jewish modernity. Furthermore, the Zionist belief that ultimately there was no collective "place" for the Jews in Europe was borne out not only by Nazism but also by the refusal of the Western democratic powers to shelter more European Jewish refugees while there was still time. And the Zionist colony in Palestine provided a base for the rescue of refugees before World War II and a place for survivors to reconstruct their lives after the war.

If the Zionist program—indeed, in its most nationalistic and antiliberal forms—seems prescient in crucial respects, its implementation seems retrograde in equally crucial ways. The Zionist program was conceived around the turn of the twentieth century, largely according to European ideologies of national liberation. The Jewish state, however, was only founded after World War II. The formation of Israel does not fit neatly into the idea of self-determination that rationalized the creation of states during decolonization—an idea shared by the (ex)colonizers and Third World nationalists alike. Israel did not come into being through the granting to a people of sovereignty in the territory they had been occupying continually since before some putative original incursion within the frame of modern European capitalist expansion. As Lord Balfour's explicit *denial* of Palestinian self-determination confirms,[1] it would better have fit the decolonizing model for the Palestinian Arabs to have been granted independence in the territory between the Mediterranean and the Jordan. But because there really was a Jewish question inherent in the political logic of Europe (which we can gloss both as a question for Jews of "Where can we go, what can we do?" and as a question for other Europeans of "Where can we send them, what can we do with them?"), that was not to be. Instead Israel came into being as a simultaneously willed *and* forced gathering of a patently reconstituted people, with a multivalent relation to imperialism and postimperialism, in a territory to which the ideologists of that group claim they are returning. Despite this "anomalous" process, an Israeli Jewish people has come into being. Its right to self-determination is granted even by representative Palestinian intellectuals, who thereby acknowledge that there are more complex grounds for self-determination than continuous territorial integrity.[2]

At the same time, this statist "solution" to Europe's Jewish problem is extremely convenient to the post–World War II heirs of imperialism. Indeed it is so convenient that, in trying to defend its moral logic, they are compulsively led to deny again and again the flaws in their own notions of polity that contributed to the crisis of Jewry, as well as the grounds of Palestinian collective identity and the merits of the Palestinian "class action suit." Thus it becomes necessary to enumerate the costs and inadequacies of the Zionist program as implemented.

First and, it seems, foremost is the cost to the people who inhabited the land the Zionists desired. Insisting on this contradicts the standard Israeli historiography about the origins of the Palestinian refugees — an account that I, like many others, passively absorbed until the Israeli invasion of Lebanon in 1982. I didn't think about it much. I suppose I would have responded to an essay question that *the "Arabs" could not tolerate the presence of powerful Jews in their midst. Therefore, when Israel declared its independence, the Arab governments invaded Israel [note that Palestine has already become Israel in this account!]. In the process of doing so, they arrogantly told the Arabs inside Israel [there is no distinction between the 1947 partition plan boundaries and the postarmistice, pre-1967 borders of Israel here] to leave for a few weeks until their armies had time to push the Jews into the sea.* I gradually became aware that this account serves very effectively to erase Palestinian ties to land inside Israel, to preclude Palestinian claims from gaining legitimacy, and to whitewash many ugly aspects of the process by which Israel came to be a state.[3] More specifically, I have learned and am finally able to take note of such things as the well over 300 Palestinian villages whose residents were exiled as a result of the 1947-49 war; of the efforts of the Zionist Executive, between the two world wars and with the connivance of the British government, to disrupt traditional patterns of Palestinian land tenure, deny Palestinians agricultural loans, and so on, and thereby accomplish their aims of acquiring control of strategic geographical regions, with the intention of setting up a Zionist state (Atran 1989); of Chaim Weizmann's denial, in a letter to Lord Balfour in 1918, that the democratic system of majority rule should be applied in Palestine, as it "does not take into account the superiority of the Jew to the Arab, the fundamental qualitative difference between Arab and Jew" (Kayyali 1978: 52).

A second cost is the repression of Jewish, rather than Israeli nationalist, cultures. Contrary to the Zionist negation of Diaspora Jewish history and culture, there were in fact countless vibrant Jewish subcultures in Europe and elsewhere that were "imported" to Israel. The official Israeli policy of assimilation rather than encouragement of diversity has resulted in a high degree of alienation from the secular nationalism of the state, alienation between immigrant generations and their children, and discrimination against successive waves of immigrants, especially against Jews who are not of European origin. The congruence between this discrimination and Weizmann's belief in "the fundamental qualitative difference between Arab and Jew" is not lost on critical Israeli Jews from Arab backgrounds. One of them, Meir Amor, has pointed out that one reason Oriental Jews seem to be the most racist of Israelis is that, in order to prove themselves *as Israelis*, they have to prove that they are *not Arabs* (Amor 1989). Further evidence that differentiation of the Jewish collective from the Arab other is a strenuous task for Israeli nationalism is the recent arrest of an Israeli Jewish educator named Arna Mer on charges of "identifying with the enemy." The specific act she was censured for was going to the Palestinian town of Jenin to provide educational materials to schoolchildren.

In regard to security, forty years after the founding of the state, the Jewish citizens of Israel do not feel physically safe. Indeed, their deeply rooted impression of insecurity itself bars Israeli Jews from dealing with Palestinian Arab neighbors[4]—a process essential to the possibility of real security and of an equitable regional economy not dependent on massive involvement with the United States.

It is an ambiguous point in favor of Zionism that, to varying degrees, Zionist thinkers anticipated the disaster of European Jewry. They could not prevent it, however. Nor do I believe that any hypothetical arguments for Israel's role in preventing a future genocide against Jews can justify the continuation of structured inequality among Israeli Jews, the second-class citizenship of Israeli Palestinians, or the occupation of Palestinian lands beyond the Green Line.

I trust that by now I have provided the context for several critical questions, which I will not attempt to answer directly here.

First, if Zionism was the only "realistic" option for the Jews and it was so patently inadequate, what are the implications for the critique of European nationalism, and why is the consistency of Zionist plans for evacuation from Europe with Nazi plans for making Europe *Judenrein* interpreted morally to condemn or to praise Zionism rather than as a symptom of a common pathology?

Second, a question expressed by a Guyanese friend of mine in the course of explaining the origins of his interest in the Jewish question:

Why did Europe feel it needed to rid itself of this particular group of people? The analogous question may equally be asked: Why does the Israeli state feel it needs to rid itself of these people? (Many Israeli Jews are sensitive to the chilling parallels to Nazi practices implicit in the recent decision of a West Bank settler community to force Palestinian workers to wear badges identifying them as "foreign workers." Indeed, there was an important symbolic protest by Israelis to this step: yellow stars were immediately produced and distributed bearing in Hebrew the words *ani oved zar*—I am a foreign worker.)

Third, why are we so reluctant to confront the impossibility of just action in the past in the terms in which the options were phrased? Within the same framework of Enlightenment and progress that we still rely on for making sense out of the course of our lives (which is a modern Christian framework),[5] we are prejudiced toward assuming that we exert sufficient control over our own environment to guarantee our basic well-being. When we see that others have failed in the past, we tend to assume it was because they understood their situation incorrectly—that there *was* a way out of their predicament, had they only seen it. This leaves a dilemma—which I will leave as a dilemma for now—between a belief that we *can* learn to shape our own history for the future and the necessary recognition that people in the past have found themselves with no possibility of action adequate to the situation.

Finally, raising the links between Zionism and the generative order of European nationalism raises the question of the premodern origins of these ideologies. To what extent can or should ancient Israel be understood as the very model of the Western nation-state? What are the grander links among the ancient Jewish state, the Western cultural complex of "Zion" through the Bible, traditional Jewish culture in the modern period, Zionism, and what I will call here a postmodern ideal of diaspora?[6] Again, I am not ready to answer this question while standing on one foot. But I think it needs to be stated, since it is a crucial element informing—usually implicitly, rarely explicitly, and then always in highly charged and debatable fashion—the intellectual rhetoric surrounding the Israeli-Palestinian "conflict."

I want to return now to the topic I began with, in order to end with something slightly more substantial than this last series of grand questions. In my valuation, the Zionist experience—largely *because of* the resistant presence of the Palestinians—indicates the dangers both of attempting to escape the complex burden of history by jumping clear toward an unburdened future, an entirely ungrounded "fresh start," and of attempting to escape history by a return to a mythic past. But how else can Jewish historicity be conceived, when the everyday grounds of Jewish collective experience have been so radically altered that there is no going back?

The Holocaust and the establishment of Israel have been described as "the Jewish return to history" (Fackenheim 1978). This is only true within a Hegelian conception of history as the history of states. If instead we view states as products of history, rather than the vehicle of history, it is altogether easy to see that Jews have been inextricably part of European and Mediterranean history for millennia, and that they would not have survived otherwise.[7] Nevertheless, if any event is epoch-making, then genocide and statehood are epochal events. In this sense I would rather claim that Israel does not objectively inaugurate, but rather existentially *demands*, a new era in Jewish history— inasmuch as history is not an external framework within which human lives are played out, but the human way of surviving (or bringing destruction) by telling stories about ourselves. Jews are now faced with the task of fundamentally refashioning our history—rearticulating our relation both to our ancestors and to our contemporaries who call themselves Jews. We face that task both among ourselves and vis-à-vis the rest of the world.

Among Jews, this demand may be described by the contradiction between the achievement of one Zionist goal and the failure to achieve another Zionist goal. The first goal, which has been problematically achieved, is "normalization"—Israelis, by and large, have the same fundamental attachment to their nation-state as citizens of other nation-states do (unhappy and conflicted as that attachment may be!). Within that system, Israeli Jews "as a nation" have shed the burden— perhaps we should say the illusion—of Jewish moral superiority and behave in much the same short-sighted way as other nations. The second goal, which has not been realized, is the ingathering of the exiles. Most Jews could move to Israel if they wanted to, and choose not to. Yet, left by the ravages of genocide and communal, cultural dismemberment with little choice but Israel as the prime focus of Jewish collective affiliation, Israel turns out to be an inadequate focus. For indeed it is "normal"; this State of Israel is not and officially does not care to be "a light unto the nations." Then how adequately can it be a light unto Jews elsewhere?

Vis-à-vis the rest of the world, despite vaunted Israeli military might — including nuclear capabilities — and the consistency with which the military needs of the Israeli state are responded to by the United States, Israel is not the United States. We Jews as a collective, and Israel as a state, cannot afford to be as blind toward the humanity of our neighbors as the United States has been. We will not be allowed to be so forever. We are not as powerful — not in that way, at least.

Along with whatever benefits Zionism has brought, its destructive effects are all related to the disastrous consequences of modern European history, and in particular of the attempt to ground collective identity in the authority of nation-states made up of culturally homogeneous groups of citizens. We (not just Jews) are going to have to do better, because we are not willing or able to give up collective identities, and allying those identities with or entrusting them to the state is sooner or later disastrous.

Ultimately, I am in favor of the "no-state" solution. The problem is, I also grant to both Israelis and Palestinians the right to self-determination, and neither is willing to give up claims to a state right now. When they get their state, Palestinians may or may not make some bad choices similar to some the Israelis have made, but they cannot be denied the chance to make those choices. Furthermore, Palestinians are clearly in the moral ascendancy right now, since they have a more authentic basis for collective identity (though not without problems, sutures that require silences) in the living memory of recent collective loss of a shared homeland and, more important, since they are at present joined together in struggle against a power that does not acknowledge their common humanity.

Israelis, on the other hand, are facing a collective identity crisis. The thrust of majority Zionism has been to "de-Judaize" the Israeli Jews while "Judaizing" the land: to strip the Jews of their collective memories, the practices and subcultures that sustained them for thousands of years, and to replace all these with secular progressivism and an ideology of the land. Discrimination against Palestinians is an inevitable consequence of that historically understandable but disastrous choice.

And if, as I contend, Zionism has become dysfunctional, then even Israelis who are aware of this are hard put to know what to replace it with.

Ideology and the local account of history are the cracking glue that binds the Israeli nation. A wave of "revisionist" historical writing about the establishment of the state and the fate of the Palestinians constitutes an implicit attempt to come to terms with the roots of the stubborn persistence of Palestinian identity. Fouad Moughrabi argues that "such a debate has little to do with the Palestinians; they only serve as a pretext for the debate" (Moughrabi 1989: 82). This raises the conundrum of whether the existence of Palestine is essential to, or merely evidence of, the statist problems inherent in Zionism. And it remains to be seen how deeply and how broadly the critique initiated in these retrospective works will extend in current politics. But I think it is fair to say that engaged scholars such as Simha Flapan are indeed searching for a way to address Palestinian humanity adequately, without completely dismantling their own historical identity (Flapan 1987).

What is on the agenda is a search for alternative strategies that Israeli Jews and Jews outside Israel could, in their various situations, adopt toward the linked problems of collective identity formation and collective security. Jews, and others who find Jewish collective existence of value in their world, must learn how to enjoy the presence of a place where Jews enjoy cultural hegemony without attempting to guarantee that situation eternally in ways that inevitably become paranoid and racist. Critics on the left especially should distinguish between deflating the idolization of Israel and demonizing Israeli Jews in turn.

In addressing these issues, I first argue for a partial withdrawal from conceptions of linear progress that inevitably impoverish Jewish identity. The concatenation of genocide and statehood in the same decade are implicitly and misleadingly framed as a dramatically telescoped progression from barbarism to rational order.[8] It is worth retaining a distinction between vectored historical narrative—a feature of the Jewish Bible that sets Judaism apart from cosmologies of the eternal return—and the triumphalist conception of inevitable progress that is inseparable from the modern version of imperial European Christianity. Understanding that we are differently situated, not smarter, than our forebears would allow Jews to bring back into our self-conception a more potent measure of the form of consciousness the cultural historian Max Weinreich called "panchrony" (Weinreich 1980). In a panchronistic world, all Jewish generations were, in a sense we find difficult even to comprehend, contemporaneous with one another. Massive pressures led to the suppression of that traditional consciousness. Right now, only a privileged few — scholars, poets, musicians, those who maintain separatist communities I might find objectionable on other grounds — have access to the resources implicit in a panchronous view. What I am suggesting is not merely a change in several individual minds but a communal reorganization that cannot take place apart from real democratization of the larger society.

The basic point remains: interaction among Jews need not be based on all Jews living together in the same *space*. If we devote more of our energies toward resurrecting our ancestors, then Jews can derive much of the interactive sustenance we need from living together in time. And, once we recognize that our ancestors were constrained much as we are, we need not feel threatened by the historical accounts of other peoples — such as the Palestinians — constituting themselves through the creation of shared memories.

I am not arguing for a new *unitary* Jewish identity. I think rather that, in order to find their voices, in order to overcome defensiveness, Jews need to exercise an infinite variety of ways to be both Jew and Other. Jews can only constitute themselves as such in relation with others who are both like and unlike them. This, in fact, is the place to acknowledge that my perspective is that of someone who chooses to remain in New York, the largest Jewish center in the world *outside* Israel — a place where Jews enjoy great cultural freedom and also constitute a well-organized polity within a declining imperial power. In Argentina, for instance, it would not be quite so easy to assert one's primary Jewish identification and simultaneously take for granted one's Argentinian identity. Whether the existence of Israel makes it harder or easier to be Jewish in a country like Argentina is not for me to say.

In regard to the corporeal well-being of Jewish persons, I argue for a planetary, rather than national or even regional, model of "security." In an unanticipated way, because there is not a neat space available for the Jews, because Jews have only been able to attain their nation-state at the cost of further displacing (and thereby helping to crystallize the consciousness of) another nation, the Jewish experience turns out to be a paradigmatic example of the inadequacy of the generative social order of nationalism. Without returning to a feudal generative order in which Jews found their greatest security as a virtual caste of cultural and economic brokers, Jews may find a renewed common purpose in their role (shared with other dispersed groups) as the yeast of social ferment. Instead of land acquisitiveness and the demographic fear that Jews may cease to be the majority in even *one* state, we Jews should recognize the strength that comes from a diversity of communal arrangements and concentrations both among Jews and with our several others. We should recognize that the copresence of those others is not a threat, but rather the condition of our own lives.

In a sense, then, the controversial prophetic vision of the global link between the fate of the Jews and the fate of the world seems to be confirmed. Jewish survival does turn out to be inseparable from human survival. Our planet more and more clearly appears as a fragile life support system rather than the plane on which a grid is drawn, within which homogeneous human groups can comfortably place themselves. This does not guarantee Jews freedom from persecution in the short term; nothing can. But it is our only chance for survival in the long term.

To employ in conclusion a mix of economic and ecological metaphor, if this analysis is plausible, Jews—and by extension others as well—are implicitly guided away from a notion of "scarcity" in competition for historical legitimacy (Appadurai 1981); away from the predominant grounding of collective identity in exclusivist territoriality; toward a notion of history as the atmosphere we all must breathe and share; and toward the nonexhaustible, but perpetually extinguishable, resources of memory.

Notes

Introduction

1. A few of the prominent discussions of the literary/theoretical issues related to Jews and genocide include Kristeva's study of the relation between anti-Semitism and "the abject" (1982); Blanchot's examination of the connection between "the writing of the disaster" and writing *as* disaster (1986); Lyotard's philosophical interrogation of "revisionist" historical claims that the gas chambers didn't exist (1988); and his *Heidegger and "the jews"* (1990).

2. One way for male critics to avoid arrogating feminist discourse is to engage feminism not only as a generalized "white male" but within a more nuanced framework of identities. In the course of a debate with Sandra Gilbert and Susan Gubar, Frank Lentricchia perhaps attempts something of this, in a polemical and parodic way, by a send-up of the stereotype of Italian immigrant machismo culture (Lentricchia 1988: 410). But where, as in that exchange, it is positions and reputations that are at stake, rather than the attempt to tell and hear of different stories, different desires, this technique will not be effective.

3. On an analogous recognition of the "double gesture" as a way to practice law without losing consciousness of law's inadequate relation to justice, see the discussion by Drucilla Cornell: "The exercise of practical reason . . . demands that we make a Derridean double gesture. We need to recognize both that thematization in law is necessary and that no thematization into a system of justice can pretend to have the last word as the truth of a 'reconstructive science' " (1990: 1705). On the temptation to believe that in oral history one can recoup the past whole, and on the inevitable recognition that this is not so, see Lapierre (1989: 30).

4. I am also looking forward to Marc Kaminsky's study "on the keyword *mentsh*" in Yiddish culture, one of the primary texts for which is Chaim Zhitlovsky's lectures on *yid* and *mentsh* (1912).

131

One   The Lower East Side:
A Place of Forgetting

1. The title of this essay is a parody of the recent massive publications *Les Lieux de mémoire* (Nora 1984). For the construction of spatially fixed memory in Israel, see the chapter entitled "An Image of a Homeland" in Benvenisti (1986: 17-46). For a discussion of spatially fixed memory used in the service of communal standards on a more intimate scale than the nation, see Basso (1984).

2. This relation is eloquently expressed by Walter Benjamin: "One might, for example, speak of an unforgettable life or moment even if all men had forgotten it. If the nature of such a life or moment required that it be unforgotten, that predicate would not imply a falsehood but merely a claim not fulfilled by men, and probably also a reference to a realm in which it *is* fulfilled: God's remembrance." (1969a:70) We could say with Benjamin, then, that the content of *oubli* is that which is forgotten by humanity but remembered by God.

3. Trent Schroyer defines domination as "socially unnecessary constraints of human freedom" (1973: 15). I flinch at the confident assertion that domination is "unnecessary," but I suppose that for my distinction between *oubli* and absence to stand, I must go along with the assumption that domination can be overcome.

4. In this regard, the philosophical insistence on absence as inherent in humanity, far from being elitist jargon, may be a useful hedge against naturalistic blood-and-soil mysticism.

5. Interestingly enough, while biblical law stipulates that inherited land is inalienable (Leviticus 25: 25-28), the Scripture takes care to avoid any mythical identification between human groups and land, relating the very prohibition against sale to God's possession: "And the land shall not be sold in perpetuity; for the land is Mine; for ye are strangers and settlers with me" (ibid., verse 23).

6. This is, of course, not true only of the Jews, nor need the implantation of this theme into a culture take centuries: "Each Palestinian structure presents itself as a potential ruin. . . . Each new house is a substitute, supplanted in turn by yet another substitute. The names of these places extend all the way from the private . . . to the official, or institutionalized, sites of ruin. . . . " (Said 1986: 30-39).

7. Courses in "how to lose your New York accent" are still offered today.

8. This concern for geography may seem odd for a people supposedly so unconcerned with physical space. But the resonances of spatial associations through time—of Jewish chronotopes—double back against each other in even more complex ways than this. There is a yeshiva in Jerusalem named after the Jewish community of Siebenburgen, in Hungary. A calendar published to promote the yeshiva bears an illustration of a city surrounded by hills and the quotation in Hebrew "yerushalayim horim soviv law" (Jerusalem is surrounded by hills), suggesting not only the identification of Siebenburgen with Jerusalem, but also an injunction to remember Siebenburgen as Jews are enjoined to remember Jerusalem, and the realization of the spiritual Siebenburgen in the earthly Jerusalem.

9. I am carefully circumlocuting *community* here, although I will use the term advisedly later on. It is hardly an objective analytic term. See the interrogation of its various meanings in the American context in Varenne (1986: 213-14).

Two **Europe's Indian, America's Jew:
Modiano and Vizenor**

1. At this point the choice of which words to place in quotation marks becomes almost completely arbitrary, symptomatic of a rare degenerative condition in which the patient is ultimately unable to sustain any pretense at critical writing.

2. Including, of course, my own. See J. Boyarin (1991).

3. Further on the link between empire building and monument building, see Henry Nash Smith's quote from a speech by Nathaniel Ames of Harvard in 1758: "Shall not . . . those vast quarries . . . that teem with mechanic Stone—those for Structure be piled into great Cities—and those for Sculpture into Statues to perpetuate the honor of renowned Heroes" (in Smith 1970: 124).

4. Specifically on the relation between egotism and egalitarianism, see Kapferer (1988: 15, 207).

5. At least part of one of May's books was translated into Yiddish in Warsaw in 1926, under the title *Der geheymer shlos*.

6. Of course German literature did not simply invent a Red Man in order to avoid acknowledging the social exclusion of its Jew or to suppress the memory of the Jewish genocide, which came long after the Red Man was invented. Such invented Others are always multifunctional. I suspect, nevertheless, that the link between the German identification with an idealized Red Man (pure, strong, living in a natural *Gemeinschaft*) and the anti-Semitic stereotype of the Jew (degenerate, weak, overly urbanized) could be articulated through research.

7. This image is inspired by stories of the *intifada* about Israelis and Palestinians evading Israeli army roadblocks to meet and express their shared desire for peace and independence.

8. I can't leave this assertion seemless, because there is also, remarkably, a growing Jewish voice and presence, especially in France, that is neither limited to intellectual circles nor inevitably obsessed with its image in non-Jewish circles (for a first approach to that phenomenon, see Friedlander 1990).

9. Several of Vizenor's books have recently been reprinted by the University of Minnesota Press. Modiano's novels have won various French literary prizes; they are discussed in an essay by Gerald Prince (1986).

10. The horror of our decades is such that viewing skeletons can sometimes be a relief. This was my reaction to viewing Dusan Makevejev's *Sweet Movie*, which interspersed documentary footage of the exhumation of the Polish officer corps at the Katyn Forest with fictional scenes of transgressive body rituals and the slaughter of children.

11. Nor is it the case that what is buried and dead is no longer potent. Past relations of violence produce skeletal aftereffects of particular force. Detouring for a moment to Argentina, we find links between the mystical, malevolent power projected onto Jews by the Argentine junta (Taussig 1984: 487) and the demonized, mystical "Indian" produced by colonizing society in general in the process of brutal subjugation.

12. Thus in contemporary Latin America a complex symbolic economy involves "lowland shamans as mythic objects to fulfill the colonially inspired mythology that grants the pagan power" of the upland shamans who cure "whites," mestizos, and other Indians (Taussig 1987: 153). I imagine the examples could be multiplied with sources from around the world.

13. In his book *Beyond Geography* (1980), Frederick W. Turner attempts to locate that originary source in the Jewish Bible. But Turner's brave attempt at a comprehensive account of the interactions among history, myth, nature, and empire suffers from a powerful anti-Jewish bias. Turner overwhelmingly valorizes myth (without distinguishing between state-empire myth and autonomous, non-class-group myth) and denigrates history (without distinguishing between the history of dominating and dominated peoples). There is no notion of collective memory in Turner's book, although since he cites Jung so often, he probably does believe in a collective unconscious. There is also no room in his account for the annual Jewish reenactments of founding historical events such as the Exodus. For Turner, the shift away from myth, polytheism, women-centered worship, harmony with nature, and ethnic tolerance toward history, monotheism, patriarchy, alienation from nature, and genocidal impulses is epitomized and encapsulated in the Hebrew Bible, conveyed (like the infectious diseases he makes much of) into the decaying Roman Empire, and thence onward and upward into modern imperial history. Turner's causal explanations as well as his categories are often anachronistic. Thus, for example, "Christianity's turn from myth toward history may have an interior historical explanation, for its first converts were Jews, as were its first authors" (62). But when "its" first converts were Jews, "it" was not yet Christianity. So in effect, Turner validates an imaginary (I'm tempted to write "mythical") original "Christianity" corrupted both by its tainted connection to the Jews and then by its ideological service of the Roman Empire. No wonder, then, that Turner describes the book as "an essay in spiritual history . . . founded on that surest of realities: the human spirit and its dark necessity to realize itself through body and place" (7). Whatever that means.

While I, too, am concerned about the connections among history, myth, nature, and empire, Turner's book seems so tendentious as to make me almost want to defend Christianity and argue for the common liberating strands of the putative "Judaeo-Christian tradition." Ironically, for someone so obsessed with the need to unmask the link between history and mastery, Turner squeezes the past 5,000 years of Western experience into a monovocal, predetermined schema. His plea for the natives is logocentric in the extreme, dangerous, and worthy of closer critical attention than I have the stomach or the stamina to give it here.

14. On "The Jew as Pariah," see Arendt (1978).

15. Although I happen not to share the belief of Frederick the Great that Hebrew is the original language, I can't resist remarking that *Ishi* means *my man* in Hebrew.

16. For a social history of the phenomenon, which demonstrates among other things that the victims of Jewish pimps were themselves Jews, see Bristow (1983).

17. The allusion here is to Herculine Barbin, a nineteenth-century French hermaphrodite who was known as Alex/Alexina (Foucault 1980a).

18. Modiano's satire anticipates in significant ways Alain Finkielkraut's exploration of the theme of "the imaginary Jew" (1980).

19. Sonnenfeld (1989), speaking on the theme of noses in Proust, has pointed out how, toward the end of *Temps*, "Marcel"/Proust mocks the idea of his own nobility.

20. Krupat (1989) sharply criticizes Momaday's monologism, which seems consistent with being more quoted than read.

21. Remember Sartre's play *No Exit*? The predominant French literary mood in 1968, of course, is still existentialism.

22. As is well known and well documented (but generally ignored by such organs as the *New York Times*), the so-called Ansar III or Ketziot prison in the Negev desert contains thousands of Palestinian men living in tents. Many of them are never formally

charged, but are held without recourse under so-called administrative detention. The legalistic rationale for their confinement dates back to the British emergency regulations imposed during the chaotic end of the British mandate after World War II.

23. These two examples of fiction preceding history cast a revealing light on Linda Hutcheon's discussion of "historiographic metafiction" as a characteristic mode of postmodernism (1988), suggesting that the phrase *metafictive history* would be just as applicable. They might also be relevant to the predicament of Salman Rushdie — clearly a case of history bites fiction.

Three　The Former Hôtel Moderne: Between Walter Benjamin and Polish Jews in Paris

1. The fieldwork discussed in this chapter was supported by a Social Science Research Council International Doctoral Research Fellowship. Marc Kaminsky gave me valuable criticism of an earlier draft.

2. For a detailed consideration of the sociology of Jewish monuments and commemoration in postwar European politics, see Young (1989).

3. This quote is taken from the *Passagen-Werk* notebook translated as "Theoretics of Knowledge, Theories of Progress" (Benjamin 1983-84: 3).

4. Jean-François Lyotard's *The Postmodern Condition* (1984).

5. In my ethnography of the immigrant community (J. Boyarin 1991), I make the claim that its form is consistent with the immigrants' own desire for a coherent narrative of their lives. This would seem to contradict Benjamin's resistance of the esthetic urge toward a seamless narrative flow. Stéphane Mosès has articulated Benjamin's resolution of this paradoxical call for a recounting of the fractured history of the oppressed: "When history takes the memory of the vanquished into account, it borrows the most specific features of tradition: its non-linearity, its breaks and interruptions, in short, the radical *negativity* manifest in it. In contrast to historical rationality, founded on the fiction of a homogeneous temporal flux linking successive instants, tradition — the transmission of a collective memory from generation to generation — most inherently implies a break from time, the fracture between eras, the gaping void separating fathers from sons. If, for Benjamin, tradition serves as a vehicle for authentic historical consciousness, it is because it is founded on the reality of death" (Mosès 1989: 15). This articulation could well serve as a critical standard for judging my ethnography, where the strongest material is contained in the chapter on funerals.

6. This is found in another draft of Benjamin's project, published as "Paris, Capital of the Nineteenth Century" (Benjamin 1978: 154).

7. It is also true, as Susan Buck-Morss points out, that Benjamin made sparing references in the *Passagen-Werk* to any specifics of the crisis of the 1930s (Buck-Morss 1989).

8. Philippe Ivernel discusses the two basic themes of Paris in Benjamin's work in a way that illuminates the two "visions" I have just outlined: "the Paris of the Capital, of dreamy lethargy, chained to the mythic forces of merchandise, of fashion . . . a negation all the more threatening to history since it takes on the appearance of history itself . . . and the Paris of revolts and revolutions, the Paris of volcanic activity, which places history on the political agenda and politics on the agenda of history" (Ivernel 1986: 252).

9. In a reverse strategy that likewise serves to domesticate the street, the department stores sell merchandise from stalls located just outside their walls.

10. This does not necessarily imply return to "primitive" conceptions. In addition to Eliade's famous *Cosmos and History: The Myth of the Eternal Return* (1959), compare de

Santillana and von Dechend (1969), which analyzes various mythologies as the poetic expressions of several civilizations' astronomical observations of heavenly cycles.

11. Baudelaire condemned boredom at the beginning of *Les Fleurs du Mal*:

> Mais parmis les chacals, les panthères, les lices,
> Les singes, les scorpions, les vautours, les serpents,
> Les monstres glapissants, hurlants, grognants, rampants,
> Dans la ménagerie infâme de nos vices,
> Il en est un plus laid, plus méchant, plus immonde! . . .
> C'est l'Ennui! (1972: 32)

12. The analogy seems closest in regard to ethnographers who work in urban settings as I do. We cannot really pretend to know the entire lives of those about whom we write, yet most of our models in the ethnographic genre are still grounded in the totalizing "village study" mode.

13. In Taussig's seminar on commodity fetishism at New York University, spring 1989. I am grateful to Professor Taussig for permitting me to attend the seminar.

14. Quoted in Aragon (1971: 14). Compare Marshall Berman's passionate account of the stroke of engineering by Robert Moses that bisected the Bronx, tore its heart out, and established the nightmarish Cross-Bronx Expressway (Berman 1988).

Four   Jewish Ethnography and the Question of the Book

1. A draft of this chapter was presented at the annual meeting of the American Ethnological Society in Santa Fe in April 1989 and another to the Proseminar on Knowledge, Culture, and Power at the Center for Studies of Social Change, New School for Social Research. It was completed while I was beginning a Social Science Research Council-MacArthur Foundation Fellowship in International Peace and Security. My thanks to Uzome Esonwanne, Michael Fischer, and Talal Asad for their comments.

2. Other major sources include writings of ancient Greeks (see Hartog 1988) and, presumably, the later Christian encounter with European "pagans." Furthermore, the rise of modern ethnology is closely linked to the problems of interpretation and belief of modern Western Christianity, a connection whose implications for the ethnographic study of Jews has been richly explored by Howard Eilberg-Schwartz (1990).

3. Thus we will beware of Gerald Bruns's claim that the hermeneutical principle implied by the question "Who has the right to say what a text means? . . . is not imperious but commonsensical" (1987: 643). It is both commonsensical and imperious. The attempt to compare and contrast Jewish and Christian hermeneutics is muddied by an apologetics that removes the question of power. Intriguingly, this defensiveness does not prevent Bruns from an insightful account of Jewish reading, which I cite near the end of this chapter.

4. The article on "Area" in the *International Encyclopedia of the Social Sciences*, while acknowledging that areas can also be located in time, goes on to state that "the adjectives 'areal' and 'spatial' . . . are most aptly used interchangeably at an abstract level in references to the distribution of phenomena over the earth's surface . . . in contrast with distributions that occur along a temporal dimension" (Ginsburg 1968: 399).

5. Ratzel was also the author of a study on *Lebensraum* (1966).

6. Two clarifications are called for here. First, while Jews have had the formal status of legal minorities in various contexts (notably the Ottoman Empire), there is a particular structure of feeling associated with the idea of a minority group in the context of

the evolution of modern European nation-states. David Lloyd (commenting on Deleuze and Guattari 1986) notes that in this context, minorities are understood as being deterritorialized, not where they belong. Their effective disenfranchisement is seen as being justified by this displacement and by their being underage, "not yet fully developed, childlike, and subject to tutelage until assimilation is accomplished" (Lloyd 1987: 175).

Second, by "wherever they live" I do mean to include the State of Israel. The minority structure of feeling, applied to the Jews, is carried over into Israel's legitimated dependency on Western Europe, especially the United States. It probably also contributes to the image of Israel as surrounded by hostile countries and blocks imagination of the possibility that Israelis could become integrated into their region without dissolving their particular identity. But more on this elsewhere.

7. A perceptive (but, alas, anonymous) journal reviewer wonders why "Louis Wirth's study of the 'ghetto' in Chicago [is] not a more notable first monument than *Life Is with People*." The example actually makes my point sharper: Wirth's work was done in sociology not anthropology, in urban studies not area studies. Hence it was not subject to quite the same genre strictures as Zborowski and Herzog's book, and it is not usually included in the same genre of ethnography. The same reviewer wonders why I exclude from my purview "historical accounts of Jews including their urban settings," such as the work of Heinrich Graetz and Salo Baron. Again, it seems precisely relevant that these are *historical* studies, as I have said, of persons "existing in time, in history." *Life Is with People* had to work against the conventional social-scientific placement of Jews in genres such as sociology and history in order to make them fit within the existing anthropological paradigm.

This is not at all to say that its subject matter or its assumptions were invalid. Indeed, the articulation of the idea of the *shtetl* has been critical to further work in Jewish ethnography. Working from a very different ethnographic setting, Michael Herzfeld makes an extremely incisive comment about the importance of studying remote places (and the *shtetl*, of course, is now remote in time): "The remote places are no less relevant than the accessible. Their relevance materializes, however, when we place our studies of them in a larger intellectual context, which we shall not do if we reject the practice of rural ethnography altogether. *Why* did the earliest ethnographers think it advisable to work in Africa, Australia, the Trobriands? Why did the Victorian traveller-folklorists only discover the 'pure Greek race' in remote islands and mountain villages? *How* do modern ethnographies shed light on national self-images? Avoiding the study of remote communities simply displaces the problem itself, and still further trivializes the voice of the already much neglected rural population" (1987: 187).

8. Wood (1968) and Ford (1970) amply document the way that World War II helped both to consolidate the systematic comparison of culture areas and to stimulate the establishment of academic area studies programs and centers.

Ford explains that the files on the Marshall Islands developed at the Institute of Human Relations at Yale—the future home of the Human Relations Area Files—"were sufficient to demonstrate that the system could be used effectively for intelligence and military government purposes" (7). After the war in the early 1950s, "the Navy, the Army, the Air Force, and the Central Intelligence Agency each contributed $50,000 a year to support research on four major areas: Southeast Asia, Europe, Northeast Asia, and the Near and Middle East" (13).

Wood, describing the situation at the time of his writing, clearly if inadvertently links area studies to neocolonialism and the Cold War: "Area centers are here to stay. Area centers satisfy direct governmental needs for area specialists. These needs in foreign-aid, educational, technical, and other programs and in intelligence and military services have grown in the last decade, and it is likely that they will not greatly decrease in the next. In Britain and France, *with the disappearance of the colonial training services themselves,* the training of area specialists in university centers and through field research becomes more essential than ever. . . . The transfer of rationale for area studies from military capabilities to other capabilities, such as that for economic development or even for susceptibility to subversion, further solidifies the place of area centers in education in the humanities and social sciences" (1968: 405–406; emphasis added).

9. The connections between the realist novel and individualism have been fairly well explored, and I have learned a great deal from Edward Said about their relations in turn to imperialism. Further links to Christianity and the Other-as-interpretand are suggested by Bruns's observation that in a specific genre of patristic hermeneutics, "the interpretation of the Scriptures becomes at the same time the medium of self-understanding and self-disclosure (not to mention self-authorization)" (1987: 635). Jabès's narratorial and personal reticence in this respect may be contrasted with the egoistic example of Marek Halter's highly popular *The Book of Abraham* (1987), which supplies a free blend of historical reconstruction and frank fiction to establish for himself an unbroken genetic and scriptural genealogy back to the fall of the Second Temple in Jerusalem.

10. Similarly, it should be clear that I am neither proposing an escape from the contingencies of everyday life into purely textual analysis nor treating culture as a text, both of which carry their own dangers. On the notion of culture as text as another spatial fixing, see Rosaldo (1989: 12). Especially relevant here are Moore's critical comments on the reification of the Bible (Jewish or Christian): "The more the temporality of the reading experience is stressed—its cumulative, successive side—the more the Bible sheds its familiar image as meaning-full object. This image achieved an unprecedented heightening with the advent and interiorization of print. In the hyperspatial object model, one which has been deeply interiorized for centuries across the span of Judaeo-Christian [?—J.B.] faiths, the Bible is conceived (speaking with sweeping generality) as having all its meaning assembled and accounted for within its covers, rather like toy soldiers in a box. But even in a moderate phenomenology of reading, the text's meanings are reconceived as being momentarily available only. . . . In a temporal model the spatially conceived text-object is robbed of its 'solidity' and is reassigned a new status as an event or temporal experience" (1989: 120).

11. In this he is like Derrida, according to Elisa New: "We crassly oversimplify, of course, if we say that Derrida 'identifies' with the Jewish tradition, finding in that tradition a will or means to power. Clearly, the deconstructionist must resist such clear logocentrism" (1988: 34). In this light, both authors' discretion regarding Jewish identity can be seen as the highest form of respect for the dead.

12. I would further risk the hypothesis that communities in positions of relative marginality or powerlessness (not necessarily both at the same time), as Jews in Diaspora have frequently been, are motivated by the demands of survival toward a relatively more nuanced and less stereotyped image of those they differ from. Of course, counterexamples immediately spring to mind; no one is free from projection. The hyphothesis could only be explored within a cross-cultural discussion of what we might call "Othering up."

13. For a set of self-reflexive essays by Jewish ethnographers, see Kugelmass (1988).

14. It is significant that Derrida here locates revelation in the Garden of Eden, rather than at Sinai or in the Holy of Holies. The primacy granted to, and nostalgic longing

for, a localized and originary Voice runs counter to Derrida's own critique of logocentrism, and the consequent privileging of "vision" lends credence to Tyler's reading of Derrida. This should remind us (Jewish critical intellectuals in particular, I suppose) not to take Derrida's texts as Gospel. In this context a comment by Alice Jardine can be read as an ironic rejoinder to Elisa New's comment cited in note 10: while "Derrida sees the Greco-Christian Dialectic as unfailingly antisemitic, and in his guerrilla warfare with Truth as the ultimate product of any dialectic. . . . Derrida's writing at times seems to be less inflecting an (older) Old Testament than reforming a (newer) New Testament. . . . Derrida doth *protest*—religiously—and asks the same of his followers" (1985: 180–81). I want to add that I am utterly unconvinced by various charges that Derrida's texts are apolitical.

15. Here I should make reference to another explanation for the absence of Jews from the standard ethnographic program. It is relevant to the linked discourses of Nazism and racial geography and to the inefficacy of more benign variants of liberal social science. With regard to Native Americans, the program of Papa Franz Boas was thorough cultural description and classification. With regard to Jews, his program, throughout the 1930s, was to demonstrate the assimilability of the Jews. Hence his research on Jews concentrated exclusively on exploding the myth of racial differences. He diverted proposals to study Jewish culture because they would have emphasized Jewish distinctiveness. For the dominated Indians who nevertheless had a place, cultural anthropology; for the Jews who had no place and needed to fit into the populations whose places they occupied, antiracist physical anthropology. (This is all summarized from Kirshenblatt-Gimblett 1987; on the political inadequacy of Boas's cultural relativism, see, for example, Gorelick 1981.)

16. Elaine Marks's proposed elaboration of this insight (forthcoming) is extremely promising. For more on the Jewish voice and presence in contemporary France, see Friedlander (1990); for an example of the Jew as exemplary absent Other, see Lyotard's discussion of justice, silence, and the Holocaust (1988).

17. This hermeneutic relation is too often taken to be entirely symmetrical (and hence depoliticized), as Brian McHale points out, commenting on the Israeli critical reception of Israeli Palestinian Hebrew writer Anton Shammas's novel *Arabesques* (McHale 1990; Shammas 1986).

I had written "the dominant *party*" here, until consulting Beryl Smalley's *The Study of the Bible in the Middle Ages* made me realize that to fix Jews and Christians as "parties" would be both wrong and inconsistent with the thrust of this essay. In fact, she traces the patristic allegorical method of Origen and Clement largely back to Philo the Jew. But Philo's situation, as Smalley summarizes it, confirms my association of allegory with empire and universalism. "Philo was a practising Jew; he represented his people on a delegation to the Roman emperor. . . . Allegory conferred a quality of universality on Jewish law and history. Philo expressed this view in a metaphor which gains in meaning if we think of its political background: the Romans had fused their conquests into a world empire. Those who interpret in the literal sense only are 'citizens of a petty state'; the allegorists are 'on the roll of citizens of a greater country, namely, this whole world' " (1964: 3). Smalley repeats Philo's metaphor on a different register, however, writing that "The allegorical interpretation marks a stage in the history of any civilized people whose literature is 'primitive' " (ibid.: 2). Maybe she is right, and the move to midrash is evidence of the reintegration of the primitive into our own lives that Stanley Diamond (1986) has called for.

My brother, Daniel Boyarin—more learned in these matters than I—has recently written a comparison of midrashic and patristic accounts of the creation of Adam and Eve, in which he demonstrates the nexus in Philo among "allegory, misogyny, contempt for the senses" (D. Boyarin n.d.: 18). He is careful to insist that he is "*not* contrasting Jewish with Christian modes of reading" and that there is much in Christian interpretation "that is midrashic in hermeneutic structure . . . (e.g., *Piers Plowman*)" (ibid.: 17). He does concur that in regard to engendering, as I am arguing in regard to ethnogenesis, "for the Fathers, one-ness is ontologically privileged in the constitution of humanity, while in the rabbinic culture, 'Man' is marked by difference, by heterogeneity, from the very beginning" (ibid.: 9).

18. Two comments may help to temper my Judeocentrism here: First, by Augustine's time, what Pagels calls "the politics of paradise" had less to do with Christianity's Jewish Other than with the mutual, and sometimes conflicting, authority of the ascendant Church and the declining Empire. Second, of course, the notion of a transcendent semiotic realm is traceable at least to Plato; unfortunately, I have nothing to say about its possible political context in ancient Greece.

19. Much as Derrida (1987)—a bit gratuitously maybe, but after all, he was asked—suggests that the goal of feminist academics should be not only to find a "place" for women's studies, but also to dismantle the entire academic ontologic of the different spaces of different disciplines.

20. Jabès states: "I have always been bound to the French language, but the place I feel I occupy in the literature of our country is not, strictly speaking, a place. It is less a writer's place than the place of a book which conforms to no category. A place circumscribed then by the book and immediately claimed by the book that succeeds it" (quoted in Motte 1990: 118).

21. This contention may be related to Daniel Boyarin's claim that "rabbinic sign theory [has been] undermined within Judaism beginning from the early middle ages and onward" (n.d.: 14).

Five   The Other Within and the Other Without

1. Relevant to this point, Avital Ronell insists that "Derrida had been listening for the murmurs of the Holocaust long before this became, for intellectuals, somewhat of a journalistic imperative" (1989: 63).

2. Howard Eilberg-Schwartz, in the introduction to a pioneering study of the historical suppression and analytic possibilities of comparative biblical anthropology, writes that "if nineteenth-century and early twentieth-century intellectuals discovered the savage in distant places, subsequent thinkers gradually learned that if savagery is to be found anywhere, it is at home among us" (1990: 23-24). If the savage was admitted to Europe in the twentieth century, what does this say about the expulsion of the Jew?

3. Orvar Loefgren has suggested that "With a grand simplification one can argue that nineteenth century Western nations with colonies tended to develop an anthropological study of primitive societies, while the ethnographical interest in countries with few or no colonies was first directed towards the 'primitives within,' the rapidly disintegrating, traditional peasant culture" (1987: 8).

4. Whether or not the Other has an independent existence at all is a controversial issue. Fabian hopes for an independent "recognition of the Other that is not limited to representations of the Other" (1990: 771). Peter Mason, following Lévinas, similarly stresses the *radical* alterity of the Other and the problem of trying "to understand the

other without using the violence of comprehension to do so" (1990: 2). Homi Bhabha, on the other hand, insists that "The 'other' is never outside or beyond us; it emerges forcefully, within cultural discourse, when we *think* we speak most intimately and indigenously 'between ourselves' " (1990: 4; also 1989). Anthony Appiah (1991) more straightforwardly warns against the danger that those living in postcolonial nations may be once again frozen into the position of the West's "radically Other." The rhetoric of radical alterity, therefore, is to be used with caution also by those who would valorize the Other.

5. Thus Ivan Strenski has suggested to me that it would be worthwhile to consider material in the nineteenth-century *Revue des Etudes Juives* in the light of Said's *Orientalism* (1978). See also the historical essays in Barbara Kirshenblatt-Gimblett's forthcoming collection *Ashkenaz*.

6. See the articles on the reception of *Holocaust* in Germany in a special issue of *New German Critique* (Herf 1980; Markovits and Hayden 1980; Zielinski 1980).

7. As James Clifford observes, "This strategy has classically involved an unquestioned claim to appear as the purveyor of truth in the text. A complex cultural experience is enunciated by an individual: *We the Tikopia* by Raymond Firth; *Nous avons mangè la forêt* by Georges Condominas; *Coming of Age in Samoa* by Margaret Mead; *The Nuer* by E. E. Evans-Pritchard" (1988c: 25).

8. Said, in response to critics who complained about his failure to discuss German Orientalism, retorts that "no one has given any reason for me to have *included* [it]" (1985: 90). If these were simply complaints that Said's groundbreaking study was not encyclopedic, he is justified in not taking them seriously. Nevertheless, given the quite different and in some ways marginal experience of German-speaking lands vis-à-vis the colonized world, a companion study of German Orientalism would be quite in order. Doubtless its elements are being produced right now.

9. Most revealing, perhaps, is the coincidence of Columbus's departure on his voyage of discovery with the completion of the *Reconquista*: "The year 1492 already symbolizes, in the history of Spain, this double movement: in this same year the country repudiates its interior Other by triumphing over the Moors in the final battle of Granada and by forcing the Jews to leave its territory; and it discovers the exterior Other, that whole America which will become Latin. We know that Columbus himself constantly links the two events" (Todorov 1985: 50). No wonder that, in Spain as in the New World, the preparations for celebrating the cinquentennial are controversial.

10. Compare a comment by the mature Marx: "The chosen people bore in their features the sign that they were the property of Jehovah" (quoted in Gilman 1986: 205). By reference to a scurrilous description in a letter from Marx to Engels about the appearance of their socialist rival, the Jew Ferdinand Lassalle, Gilman suggests that these are visible, external features, such as dark skin. I wonder whether Marx might not have been referring instead to circumcision.

11. Significantly, the fragment about the animal breaks off precisely at the point where it is becoming a *story*: "Many years ago, so it is recounted, attempts were really still made to drive the animal away. The beadle of the synagogue says he remembers how his grandfather, who was also beadle, liked to tell the story. As a small boy his grandfather had frequently heard talk about the impossibility of getting rid of the animal; and so, fired with ambition and being an excellent climber, one bright morning when the whole synagogue, with all its nooks and crannies, lay open in the sunlight, he had sneaked in, armed with a rope, a catapult, and a crookhandled stick" (1961: 59).

It is unimportant whether Kafka originally intended to continue and found that the writing no longer interested him, or whether he intended precisely to suggest that positive storytelling was not the point here. What matters is that Kafka shows himself stopping just when narrative begins. Compare the ending of Sholem-Aleykhem's story "Stantsye Baranovitsh," where a complicated tale of the narrator's grandfather is interrupted just as, according to the narrator, it is about to begin (see J. Boyarin 1986).

12. Although, as Pierre Vidal-Nacquet notes, "l'exil rend lucide" (1982: 21).

Six   The Impossible International

1. A note on the history of this chapter: During the summer of 1988 I participated in two courses at the School of Criticism and Theory at Dartmouth College: Nancy K. Miller's on "The Subjects of Feminist Criticism" and Edward W. Said's on "Methodologies of Empire." The issues I take up here are related to the two professors' respective foci (as animated, to a large extent, by my fellow students) on the subject in feminism and on the role of literature in imperialist and anti-imperialist discourse. While my wife, Elissa Sampson, was left in New York City to cope with both her full-time corporate job and our two-year-old child, Jonah, I argued about critical theory and swam in the Connecticut River to relieve the heat of that greenhouse summer. This essay is largely an attempt to account for that summer of privilege. My thanks to Richard Dellamora, Robert Latham, Kitty Holland, Eloise Linger, and Charles Tilly for helping me work through to this partial articulation.

2. Gloria Watkins writes under the name of bell hooks, her great-grandmother, building on and complicating the tradition shared by immigrant Jews and African slaves of naming children after a deceased ancestor (Gutman 1977). Her strategy of commemoration through pseudonym can also be compared with the decision of "Alexander Donat," author of a powerful survivor memoir called *The Holocaust Kingdom* (1963), to adopt the name of a young man with whom he had switched identities in a concentration camp—a choice that contributed to his survival and the death of the "real" Alexander Donat.

3. The "difference" of Jewish women is, of course, not the same as the "difference" of Jewish men, as Babel's contrasting invocation of his grandfather reading Ibn Ezra while his grandmother reads fortunes in melting wax reminds us. Jewish women are, of course, included in the implied contestatory fellowship of the nonwhite, nonmale, and/or non-Western, but again, the Jewish dimension of their being "Jewish women" is often either occluded or denigrated by a movement that tends to see the Bible as the source of patriarchy and sexism. Part of the reason for this, once again, is that Jewish women as such are often perceived to be part of the elite by those who belong to groups acknowledged to be marginalized or oppressed. Nancy Miller's unpublished seminar paper presented to the School of Criticism and Theory in 1988 documented some of the painful encounters this has entailed. The silencing of the Jewish woman as a subject in/of feminist theory is documented in Beck (1988). The outline of a critique of anti-Jewish bias in Christian feminist writing is contained in Heschel (1990). More generally on issues facing Jewish feminists, see Kaye/Kantrowitz and Klepfisz (eds., 1989) and the journal *Lilith*.

4. As would a systematic comparison of the situation of Jews inside modern Europe with that of Jews in the colonies. For a discussion of the Jews of the Russian Empire as an internally colonized group, see Peled 1989 (Peled draws heavily on the model provided by Hechter 1975). Given that in the classic colonial situation, we think of the col-

onized as generally being segregated and confined to the hinterlands, it is ironic that a series of decrees in the nineteenth century forced Jews in the Russian Empire off the land and into the cities (see, e.g., Mendelsohn 1970).

5. Bizarre because of the way Freud treats the biblical text as a distorted account of a "real" history; for Freud, Moses was "really" an Egyptian. Freud's text simultaneously reifies and denigrates both the figure of Moses and the Bible narrative. Freud expresses his own ambivalence about following up on his hypothesis thus: "It is not attractive to be classed with the scholastics and Talmudists who are satisfied to exercise their ingenuity, unconcerned how far removed their conclusions may be from the truth" (1967: 17). Not that this exhausts the interest of *Moses and Monotheism*, which has served as the topic for recent lectures by scholars as diverse as Barbara Johnson (at Cardozo Law School in 1989) and Yosef Haim Yerushalmi (at Yale in the spring of 1990). I was unable to attend Professor Yerushalmi's lectures, although some of his remarks on Freud have been published before (Yerushalmi 1988). Professor Johnson's was particularly exciting because of the way she juxtaposed the Moses-as-Egyptian theme in *Moses and Monotheism* and in Zora Neale Hurston's *Moses: Man of the Mountain* (1984). Johnson linked Freud's and Hurston's displacement of Moses' "organic" connection as a heroic leader of his people to the two writers' own ambivalent relation to the identity and struggles of European Jewry and African-Americans — precisely the kind of comparative critical research I am calling for here.

6. Walter Benjamin argued that "the current amazement that the things we are experiencing are 'still' possible in the twentieth century is *not* philosophical. This amazement is not the beginning of knowledge — unless it is the knowledge that the view of history which gives rise to it is untenable" (1969b: 257).

7. The heritage of this ambiguous reckoning, I suspect, lies not only in German and other nationalist resentments. The "leftist" connections of the "revisionist" Faurisson are well known (Finkielkraut 1982). The ultraleftist anti-Israelism of some Germans born after the war might also be linked, in a complicated way, to the rhetorical incorporation of the victimized "Jewish people" into a continuing structure of European domination.

8. Unlike other wild claims I make from time to time, I have an "authoritative" basis for this one in a recent lecture by Amos Funkenstein: "If we look, in the history of Christianity, for a definite class which saw it as its task to examine traditions and to criticize accepted conventions, we ought to advance to the Middle Ages, to the beginnings of universities in the 13th century. Members of the universities defended . . . their right to teach and discuss every topic (*libertas disputandi*), a right they had under the condition that they not decide any dogma or Church-teachings. . . . Time and again, university teachers are summoned to trials and asked: did you not say such-and-such? And they would often answer, I said it, but I did so *disputandi more, non asserendi more* and this is my right and privilege. Here lies the origin of the self-consciousness of intellectuals as a group called upon to examine, criticize, to look at rational alternatives in the interpretation of texts and options" (1989b: 10–11).

9. As Judith Butler puts it, "The theories of feminist identity that elaborate predicates of color, sexuality, ethnicity, class, and able-bodiedness invariably close with an embarrassed 'etc.' at the end of the list" (1990: 143).

10. This does not mean that Fascism per se is the rule; as Foucault warned, "The non-analysis of fascism is one of the most important political facts of the past thirty years. It enables fascism to be used as a floating signifier, whose function is essentially that of denunciation" (Foucault 1980b: 139).

11. Note that the making of this list is not a neutral act. One way to begin to work through the contradiction between the violence of listing and the need for naming victims might be to point out that these names differ widely in their origins and affect. Thus during the period of Nazi persecution, nearly all those persecuted as radicals would have claimed that identity; many but not all those called Jews would have called themselves Jews; some, but probably not most, of those designated "sexual deviants" would have described themselves as such, etc.

12. One would also want to look at the essay by Cixous that I criticized earlier, to reopen much more carefully an approach to comparative studies of the relation between domination on one hand and ideologies of inaccesible authority on the other.

13. And you thought the era of master narratives was over!

14. Laura Kipnis has noticed this correlation: "The theoretical emergence of these political spaces now being described by continental feminists parallels the narrative of the decline of the great imperial powers of modernity, the liquidation of the European empires and the postcolonial rearrangements of the traditional centers on a world scale" (1989: 161). I do not mean to suggest, however, that Irigaray or other feminist critics of rigid masculine subjectivity are engaging in a defense of pluralism per se. To do so would betray the substantial critique of liberal pluralism that has taken place partly within feminist theory. On the other hand, I think it is also fair to say that what might be called pluralism both in France and in the United States is more profoundly interventionist in the former state than in the latter. In France, it contests the idea that the French language and civilization are that to which all "men" should aspire; in the United States, it too often reconfirms the construction of hegemony on the trope of a nation of immigrants. For just one discussion of a proposed ethic of contentious pluralism in the United States academy, see Graff (1990).

15. The way that Jewish difference still marks the cracks in liberal theory is demonstrated by an excerpt from a recent essay by Charles Taylor. Taylor, attempting to explain the unique historical circumstances that produced Western ideas of civil society, writes that "one of the most important features of Latin Christendom . . . was the development of the idea of the Church as an independent society. In principle, the inhabitants of Christendom were Christians. But these same people were organized in two societies—one temporal, one spiritual—of which neither could be simply subordinated to the other. . . . Western Christendom was in its essence bi-focal" (1990: 102). How embarrassing it must be for Taylor to be reminded that in reality if not "in principle," some of the "inhabitants of Christendom" weren't even Christians! Western Christendom may have been bifocal in its "essence," but evidently it was also partially blind.

16. On genetics as a "historical" narrative, see Holquist (1989).

Seven   Palestine and Jewish History

1. Balfour stated in February 1919 that "in the case of Palestine we deliberately and rightly decline to accept the principle of self-determination" (Kayyali 1978). The idea that imperial powers had the "right" to "decline to accept" self-determination in any given case is a classic example of the ambiguity of universalist principles propagated by the dominant center.

2. This acknowledgment of the Israeli Jews' right to self-determination contributes to, but is not identical with, the PLO's political recognition of the State of Israel.

3. I do not mean to imply that the opposite of everything in italics here is "the real truth," which would make the Arab governments passive victims of Israeli aggression.

The Arab refusal of the partition plan is understandable, especially in light of the discrepancy between the percentage of the total population consisting of Jews and the percentage of the land granted to the Jewish homeland. However, the Palestinian cause was doomed by Arab disunity and the failure to realize that the *yishuv* was already soundly established and strategically prepared for military victory.

4. This kind of positive feedback loop between ethnic stereotypes and interethnic tensions, which characterizes many such situations, is well analyzed by Robert J. Lifton (1983).

5. I rely especially on Roy Harvey Pearce's discussion of this point: "The grand intention of the eighteenth-century Scottish historians and writers on society—among them, Francis Hutcheson, Thomas Reid, Adam Ferguson, Lord Kames, and Robertson—was to construct a sociology of progress, a theory which would make comprehensible at once social stability and social growth, which would explain to Christians how they could originally have fallen and yet have come to such a high and noble state in their enlightened century. The Scots' thinking had evolved ultimately out of a Protestant theology in which the millennium had been rationalized from a certainty of the second coming of Christ into a certainty of the God-ordained, intelligent self-sufficiency of modern man to work out his own way with his common sense, his analytic reason, and his special moral sense" (1988: 82).

6. Feminists, deconstructionist critics, and transnational migrants have all contributed toward the still-tentative formulation of this postmodern ideal of diaspora. Briefly, I would say that it regards fragmentation and ambiguity in identity, language, and history as both inevitable and enabling, not accidental and debilitating. Thus it would tend to draw on the persistence of various and partial, yet interconnected, Jewish identities as one of its models. See, for one attempt at a political program based on this ideal, Marienstras (1975).

7. A passage in a late interview between Jean-Paul Sartre and Benny Levy is instructive here. Sartre says, "Because, at the moment when I said that there is not any Jewish history, I was thinking of history in a well-defined form: the history of Germany, the history of America, of the United States. That is, the history of a sovereign, political reality with a homeland and with other similar states. When one should have thought of history as being something else, if one meant that there is a Jewish history. It was necessary to conceive of Jewish history not only as a dissemination of Jews throughout the world, but also as the unity of the diaspora, the unity of the dispersed Jews" (Levy 1980: 178). See also Fernand Braudel's almost polemical emphasis on the coherence and distinctiveness of Jewish civilization (1976: 802–25).

8. My argument here, as elsewhere, overlaps in many respects with that of Dan Diner (1983).

Bibliography

Adorno, Rolena. 1986. *Guaman Poma: Writing and Resistance in Colonial Peru*. Austin: University of Texas Press.

Amor, Meir. 1989. "The Ashkenazi-Palestinian War." *Israel and Palestine* 153 (October):15-18.

Anderson, Benedict. 1983. *Imagined Communities: Reflections on the Origin and Spread of Nationalism*. London: Verso.

Appadurai, Arjun. 1981. "The Past as a Scarce Resource." *Man (NS)* 16:201-19.

Appiah, Kwame Anthony. 1991. "Is the Post- in Postmodernism the Post- in Postcolonial?" *Critical Inquiry* 17 (Winter):336-57.

Aragon, Louis. 1971. *Paris Peasant*. London: Pan.

Arendt, Hannah. 1978. *The Jew as Pariah: Jewish Identity and Politics in the Modern Age*. New York: Grove.

Atran, Scott. 1989. "The Surrogate Colonization of Palestine, 1917-1939." *American Ethnologist* 17:719-44.

Auster, Paul. 1985. "Book of the Dead: An Interview with Edmond Jabès." In *The Sin of the Book: Edmond Jabès*, ed. Eric Gould, 3-25. Lincoln: University of Nebraska Press.

Babel, Isaac. 1955. *The Collected Stories*. New York: Criterion.

Bakhtin, Mikhail. 1981. "Forms of Time and of the Chronotope in the Novel." In *The Dialogic Imagination*, ed. and trans. Michael Holquist, trans. Caryl Emerson, 84-258. Austin: University of Texas Press.

Barker, Francis, Peter Hulme, Margaret Iverson, and Diane Loxley, eds. 1985. *Europe and Its Others*. 2 vols. Colchester: University of Essex Press.

Baron, Salo. 1964. *History and Jewish Historians: Essays and Addresses*. Ed. Arthur Hertzberg and Leon A. Feldman. Philadelphia. Jewish Publication Society.

Basso, Keith. 1984. "Stalking with Stories: Names, Places and Moral Narratives among the Western Apache." In *Text, Play and Story: The Construction and Reconstruction of Self and Society*, ed. Edward Bruner, 19-53. Washington, D.C.: American Ethnological Society.

Baudelaire, Charles. 1972. *Les Fleurs du mal*. Paris: Gallimard.

Baudet, Henri. 1965. *Paradise on Earth: Some Thoughts on European Images of Non-European Man*. New Haven, Conn.: Yale University Press.

Bauman, Zygmunt. 1988. "Exit Visas and Entry Tickets: Paradoxes of Jewish Assimilation." *Telos* 77:45-77.

Beck, Evelyn Torton. 1988. "The Politics of Jewish Invisibility." *NWSA Journal* 1:93-102.

Belke, Ingrid, ed. 1971. *Moritz Lazarus und Herman Steinthal: Die Begründer der Völkerpsychologie in ihren Briefen*. Mit einer Einleitung herausgegeben von Ingrid Belke. Tübingen: Mohr.

Benjamin, Walter. 1969a. *Illuminations*. New York: Schocken.

———. 1969b. "Theses on the Philosophy of History." In *Illuminations*, trans. Harry Zohn, ed. Hannah Arendt. New York: Schocken.

———. 1973. *Charles Baudelaire: A Lyric Poet in the Era of High Capitalism*. London: New Left Books.

———. 1978. "Surrealism: The Last Snapshot of the European Intelligentsia." 177-92. New York: Harcourt Brace Jovanovich.

———. 1983. *Das Passagen-Werk*. Frankfurt am Main: Suhrkamp.

———. 1983-84. "Theoretics of Knowledge, Theories of Progress." *Philosophical Forum* 5(1-2):1-40.

Benvenisti, Meron. 1986. *Conflicts and Contradictions*. New York: Villard.

Berger, Harry. 1989. "The Lie of the Land: The Text Beyond Canaan." *Representations* 25:119-38.

Berkhofer, Robert F. 1979. *The White Man's Indian*. New York: Knopf.

Berman, Marshall. 1988. *All That Is Solid Melts into Air: The Experience of Modernity*. New York: Penguin.

Bhabha, Homi. 1989. "Remembering Fanon: Self, Psyche, and the Colonial Condition." In *Remaking History*, ed. Barbara Kruger and Phil Mariani, 131-48. Seattle: Bay Press.

———. 1990. "Introduction." In *Nation and Narration*, ed. Homi K. Bhabha, 1-7. New York: Routledge.

Blanchot, Maurice. 1985. "Interruptions." In *Edmond Jabès: The Sin of the Book*, ed. Eric Gould, 43-51. Lincoln: University of Nebraska Press.

———. 1986. *The Writing of the Disaster*. Lincoln: University of Nebraska Press.

Borofsky, Robert. 1987. *Making History: Pukapukan and Anthropological Constructions of Knowledge*. Cambridge: Cambridge University Press.

Boyarin, Daniel. Forthcoming. *Carnal Israel: Gender, Sex and the Body in Rabbinic Judaism*. Berkeley: University of California Press.

———. 1990. *Intertextuality and the Reading of Midrash*. Bloomington: Indiana University Press.

———. n.d. "Creating Eve Differently: Midrash and Misogyny." Unpublished paper.

Boyarin, Daniel, and Jonathan Boyarin. 1989. "Toward a Dialogue with Edward Said." *Critical Inquiry* 15(3): 626-33.

Boyarin, Jonathan. 1986. "Sholem-Aleykhem's *Stantsye Baranovitsh*." In *Identity and Ethos: A Festschrift for Sol Liptzin*, ed. Mark Gelber, 89-99. New York: Peter Lang.

———. 1988. "Waiting for a Jew: Marginal Redemption at the Eighth Street Shul." In *Between Two Worlds: Ethnographic Essays on American Jews*, ed. Jack Kugelmass, 52-77. Ithaca, N.Y.: Cornell University Press.

_____. 1989. "Voices Around the Text: The Ethnography of Reading at Mesivta Tifereth Jerusalem." *Cultural Anthropology* 4:399-421.

_____. 1990. "Observant Participation: The Ethnography of Jews on the Lower East Side." *YIVO Annual* 19:233-54.

_____. 1991. *Polish Jews in Paris: The Ethnography of Memory*. Bloomington: Indiana University Press.

Braudel, Fernand. 1976. *The Mediterranean World*. New York: Harper and Row.

Bristow, Edward J. 1983. *Prostitution and Prejudice: The Jewish Fight Against White Slavery 1870-1939*. New York: Schocken.

Bruns, Gerald. 1987. "Midrash and Allegory." In *The Literary Guide to the Bible*, ed. Robert Alter and Frank Kermode, 625-46. Cambridge, Mass.: Harvard University Press (Belknap).

Buck-Morss, Susan. 1989. *The Dialectics of Seeing: Walter Benjamin and the Arcades Project*. Cambridge, Mass.: MIT Press.

Butler, Judith. 1990. *Gender Trouble: Feminism and the Subversion of Identity*. New York: Routledge.

Campbell, Mary B. 1988. *The Witness and the Other World: Exotic European Travel Writing, 400-1600*. Ithaca, N.Y.: Cornell University Press.

Carter, Paul. 1989. *The Road to Botany Bay*. Chicago: University of Chicago Press.

Césaire, Aimè. 1972. *Discourse on Colonialism*. New York: Monthly Review Press.

_____. 1983. *Collected Poems*. Berkeley: University of California Press.

Cheyfitz, Eric. 1990. *The Poetics of Imperialism: Translation and Colonization from* The Tempest *to* Tarzan. New York: Oxford University Press.

Cixous, Hélène, and Catherine Clément. 1986. *The Newly Born Woman*. Trans. Betsy Wing. Minneapolis: University of Minnesota Press.

Clifford, James. 1988a. "On Ethnographic Self-fashioning: Conrad and Malinowski." In *The Predicament of Culture: Twentieth-century Ethnography, Literature, and Art*, 92-113. Cambridge, Mass.: Harvard University Press.

_____. 1988b. "On *Orientalism*." In *The Predicament of Culture: Twentieth-century Ethnography, Literature, and Art*, 255-76. Cambridge, Mass.: Harvard University Press.

_____. 1988c. "On Ethnographic Authority." In *The Predicament of Culture: Twentieth-Century Ethnography, Literature and Art*, 21-54. Cambridge, Mass.: Harvard University Press.

Cornell, Drucilla. 1990. "From the Lighthouse: The Promise of Redemption and the Possibility of Legal Interpretation." *Cardozo Law Review* 2(5-6):1687-714.

Cornell, Stephen. 1988. *The Return of the Native: American Indian Political Resurgence*. Ithaca, N.Y.: Cornell University Press.

Dan, Joseph. 1986. "Midrash and the Dawn of Kabbalah." In *Midrash and Literature*, ed. Geoffrey H. Hartman and Sanford Budick, 127-40. New Haven, Conn.: Yale University Press.

Davies, W. D. 1982. *The Territorial Dimension of Judaism*. Berkeley: University of California Press.

de Certeau, Michel. 1980. "Writing vs. Time: History and Anthropology in the Works of Lafitau." *Yale French Studies* 59:37-64.

de Santillana, Giorgio, and Hertha von Dechend. 1969. *Hamlet's Mill*. Boston: David Godine.

Deleuze, Gilles, and Félix Guattari. 1986. *Kafka: Toward a Minor Literature*. Trans. Dana Polan. Minneapolis: University of Minnesota Press.

Der Derian, James. 1989. "The Boundaries of Knowledge and Power in International Relations." In *International/Intertextual Relations: Postmodern Readings of World Politics*, ed. James Der Derian and Michael Shapiro, 3–10. Lexington, Mass.: Heath.

Derrida, Jacques. 1976. "The Question of the Book." In *Writing and Difference*, 64–78. Chicago: University of Chicago Press.

———. 1987. "Women in the Beehive: A Seminar with Jacques Derrida." In *Men in Feminism*, ed. Alice Jardine and Paul Smith, 189–203. New York: Methuen.

Diamond, Stanley. 1986 [1974]. *In Search of the Primitive: A Critique of Civilization*. New Brunswick, N.J.: Transaction Books.

Diner, Dan. 1983. "Israel and the Trauma of the Mass Extermination." *Telos* 57 (Fall):41–52.

Donat, Alexander. 1963. *The Holocaust Kingdom*. New York: Holocaust Library.

Driver, Harold E. 1970. "Statistical Studies of Continuous Geographical Distribution." In *A Handbook of Method in Cultural Anthropology*, ed. Raoul Narroll and Ronald Cohen, 620–39. New York: Columbia University Press.

Eilberg-Schwartz, Howard. 1990. *The Savage in Judaism*. Bloomington: Indiana University Press.

Eliade, Mircea. 1959. *Cosmos and History: The Myth of the Eternal Return*. New York: Harper.

Esonwanne, Uzo. 1990–91. "The Madness of Africa(ns); or, Anthropology's Reason." *Cultural Critique* 17:107–26.

Fabian, Johannes. 1983. *Time and the Other*. New York: Columbia University Press.

———. 1990. "Presence and Representation: The Other and Anthropological Writing." *Critical Inquiry* 16:753–72.

Fackenheim, Emil. 1978. *The Jewish Return into History: Reflections in the Age of Auschwitz and a New Jerusalem*. New York: Schocken.

Finkielkraut, Alain. 1980. *Le Juif imaginaire*. Paris: Le Seuil.

———. 1982. *L'Avenir d'une negation*. Paris: Le Seuil.

Fischer, Michael M. J., and Mehdi Abedi. 1989. "Qur'anic Dialogues: Islamic Poetics and Politics for Muslims and for Us." In *The Interpretation of Dialogue*, ed. Tullio Maranhao, 120–53. Chicago: University of Chicago Press.

Flapan, Simha. 1987. *The Birth of Israel: Myths and Realities*. New York: Pantheon.

Ford, Clellan S. 1970. *Human Relations Area Files: 1949-1969*. New Haven, Conn.: Human Relations Area Files.

Foucault, Michel. 1980a. *Herculin Barbin: Being the Recently Discovered Memoirs of a Nineteenth-Century French Hermaphrodite*. Trans. Richard McDougall. New York: Pantheon.

———. 1980b. *Power/Knowledge*. Ed. Colin Gordon. New York: Pantheon.

———. 1980c. "Questions on Geography." In *Power/Knowledge*, ed. Colin Gordon, 63–77. New York: Pantheon.

Frazier, Ian. 1989. *Great Plains*. New York: Farrar, Straus & Giroux.

Freud, Sigmund. 1967 [1939]. *Moses and Monotheism*. New York: Random House.

Friedlander, Judith. 1990. *Vilna on the Seine*. New Haven, Conn.: Yale University Press.

Funkenstein, Amos. 1989a. "Collective Memory and Historical Consciousness." *History and Memory* 1(1):5–26.

———. 1989b. "Intellectuals and Jews." The Albert T. Bilgray Lecture, University of Arizona. Tucson: Temple Emanu-El.

Gates, Henry Louis, Jr. 1987. "Authority, (white) Power and the (black) Critic: It's All Greek to Me." *Cultural Critique* 7:19–46.

Gilman, Sander. 1985. *Pathology and Difference*. Ithaca, N.Y.: Cornell University Press.
———. 1986. *Jewish Self-Hatred: Anti-Semitism and the Hidden Language of the Jews*. Baltimore: Johns Hopkins University Press.
Ginsburg, Norton. 1968. "Area." In *International Encyclopedia of the Social Sciences, vol. 1*, 398–401. New York: Macmillan and Free Press.
Glatzer, Nahum, ed. 1962. *Hammer on the Rock: A Midrash Reader*. New York: Schocken.
Godzich, Wlad. 1988. "Emergent Literature and the Field of Comparative Literature." In *The Comparative Approach to Literature: Approaches to Theory and Practice*, ed. Clayton Koelb and Susan Noakes, 18–36. Ithaca, N.Y.: Cornell University Press.
Goldberg, Harvey. 1977. "Culture and Ethnicity in the Study of Israeli Society." *Ethnic Groups* 1:163–86.
González-Echevarria, Roberto. 1987. "The Law of the Letter: Garcilaso's *Commentaries* and the Origins of the Latin American Narrative." *Yale Journal of Criticism* 1(1):107–32.
Gorelick, Sherry. 1981. *City College and the Jewish Poor*. New Brunswick, N.J.: Rutgers University Press.
Graff, Gerald. 1990. "Other Voices, Other Rooms: Organizing and Teaching the Humanities Conflict." *New Literary History* 21:817–40.
Greenblatt, Stephen. 1990. "Marx, Marlowe and Anti-Semitism." In *Learning to Curse: Essays in Early Modern Culture*, 40–58. New York: Routledge.
Greer, Rowan A. 1986. "The Christian Bible and Its Interpretation." In *Early Biblical Interpretation*, ed. James L. Kugel and Rowan A. Greer, 107–208. Philadelphia: Westminster.
Gutman, Herbert. 1977. *The Black Family in Slavery and Freedom, 1770-1925*. New York: Pantheon.
Halter, Marek. 1987. *The Book of Abraham*. New York: Dell.
Handelman, Susan. 1982. *Slayers of Moses: The Emergence of Rabbinic Tradition in Modern Literary Theory*. Albany: State University of New York Press.
———. 1985. " 'Torments of an Ancient Word': Edmond Jabès and the Rabbinic Tradition." In *The Sin of the Book: Edmond Jabès*, ed. Eric Gould, 55–91. Lincoln: University of Nebraska Press.
Hanning, Robert. 1966. *The Vision of History in Early Britain: From Gildas to Geoffrey of Monmouth*. New York and London: Columbia University Press.
Haraway, Donna. 1989. *Primate Visions*. New York: Routledge.
Hartman, Geoffrey, and Sanford Budick, eds. 1986. *Midrash and Literature*. New Haven, Conn.: Yale University Press.
Hartog, François. 1988. *The Mirror of Herodotus: The Representation of the Other in the Writing of History*. Berkeley: University of California Press.
Hartsock, Nancy. 1987. "Rethinking Modernism: Minority vs. Majority Theories." *Cultural Critique* 7:187–206.
Harvey, David. 1989. *The Condition of Postmodernity*. Cambridge, Mass.: Blackwell.
Hechter, M. 1975. *Internal Colonialism: The Celtic Fringe in British National Development 1576-1966*. London: Routledge and Kegan Paul.
Hegel, G. W. F. 1977. *Early Theological Writings*. Philadelphia: University of Pennsylvania Press.
Herf, Jeffrey. 1980. "The 'Holocaust' Reception in West Germany: Right, Center and Left." *New German Critique* 19:30–52.

Herzfeld, Michael. 1987. *Anthropology through the Looking-glass: Critical Ethnography in the Margins of Europe*. New York: Cambridge University Press.

Heschel, Susannah. 1990. "Anti-Semitism in Christian Feminist Theology." *Tikkun* 5(5):25-28ff.

Hohendahl, Peter Uwe. 1989. "Von der Rothaut Zum Edelmenschen: Karl Mays Amerikaromane." In *Karl Mays Winnetou: Studien zu einem Mythos*, ed. Dieter Sudhoff and Hartmut Vollmer, 214-38. Frankfurt am Main: Suhrkamp.

Holquist, Michael. 1989. "From Body-talk to Biography: The Chronobiological Bases of Narrative." *Yale Journal of Criticism* 3(1):1-35.

hooks, bell. 1990. *Yearning: Race, Gender and Cultural Politics*. Boston: South End Press.

Horkheimer, Max, and Theodor Adorno. 1972. *Dialectic of Enlightenment*. New York: Seabury Press.

Hurston, Zora Neale. 1984. *Moses: Man of the Mountain*. Urbana and Chicago: University of Illinois Press.

Hutcheon, Linda. 1988. *A Poetics of Postmodernism: History, Theory, Fiction*. New York: Routledge.

Irigaray, Luce. 1985. "Any Theory of the Subject Has Already Been Appropriated by the Masculine." In *Speculum of the Other Woman*, 133-46. Ithaca, N.Y.: Cornell University Press.

Ivernel, Philippe. 1986. "Paris capitale du front populaire ou la vie posthume du XIXe siècle." In *Walter Benjamin et Paris*, ed. Heinz Wissman, 249-72. Paris: Le Cerf.

Jabès, Edmond. 1976. *The Book of Questions*. Middletown, Conn.: Wesleyan University Press.

_____. 1977. *Return to the Book*. Trans. Rosemarie Waldrop. Middletown, Conn.: Wesleyan University Press.

_____. 1980. *Du Desert au livre: Entretiens avec Marcel Cohen*. Paris: Belfond.

_____. 1985. "There Is Such a Thing as Jewish Writing and at This Unsuspected Boundary." In *Edmond Jabès: The Sin of the Book*, ed. Eric Gould, 26-34. Lincoln: University of Nebraska Press.

_____. 1986. "The Key." In *Midrash and Literature*, ed. Geoffrey Hartman and Sanford Budick, 349-60. New Haven, Conn.: Yale University Press.

Jardine, Alice. 1985. *Gynesis: Configurations of Women and Modernity*. Ithaca, N.Y.: Cornell University Press.

Jean-Klein, Iris E. F. 1988. Zionist Perceptions of Nazareth, Jewish Perceptions of Jew and Arab in Upper Nazareth. M. A. thesis, Memorial University of Newfoundland.

Jehlen, Myra. 1986. *American Incarnation: The Individual, the Nation and the Continent*. Cambridge, Mass.: Harvard University Press.

Kafka, Franz. 1961. *Parables and Paradoxes*. New York: Schocken.

_____. 1970. *The Great Wall of China*. New York: Schocken.

_____. 1976 [1953]. *Letter to His Father*. New York: Schocken.

_____. 1979. *The Basic Kafka*. New York: Simon and Schuster.

Kapferer, Bruce. 1988. *Legends of People, Myths of State: Violence, Intolerance, and Political Culture in Sri Lanka and Australia*. Washington, D.C.: Smithsonian Institution Press.

Kaplan, Alice Yaeger. 1989. "Theweleit and Spiegelman: Of Mice and Men." In *Remaking History*, ed. Barbara Kruger and Phil Mariani, 151-72. Seattle: Bay Press.

Kaye/Kantrowitz, Melanie, and Irena Klepfisz, eds. 1989. *The Tribe of Dina: A Jewish Women's Anthology*. Boston: Beacon.

Kayyali, Abdul-Wahhab Said. 1978. *Palestine: A Modern History*. London: Croom Helm.

Kelber, Werner H. 1983. *The Oral and the Written Gospel: The Hermeneutics of Speaking and Writing in the Synoptic Tradition, Mark, Paul, and Q.* Philadelphia: Fortress.

_____. 1989. "Narrative as Interpretation and Interpretation of Narrative: Hermeneutical Reflections on the Gospels." In *The Interpretation of Dialogue,* ed. Tullio Maranhao, 75-98. Chicago: University of Chicago Press.

Kern, Stephen. 1983. *The Culture of Time and Space, 1880-1918.* Cambridge, Mass.: Harvard University Press.

Kipnis, Laura. 1988. "Feminism: The Political Conscience of Postmodernism?" In *Universal Abandon? The Politics of Postmodernism,* ed. Andrew Ross, 149-66. Minneapolis: University of Minnesota Press.

Kirshenblatt-Gimblett, Barbara. Forthcoming. *Ashkenaz: Essays in Jewish Folkloristics.*

_____. 1987. "Erasing the Subject: Franz Boas and the Anthropological Study of Jews in the United States." Paper presented at the annual meeting of the American Anthropological Association, Chicago.

Koonz, Claudia. 1987. *Mothers in the Fatherland: Women, the Family, and Nazi Politics.* New York: St. Martin's.

Kramer, Jane. 1980. *Unsettling Europe.* New York: Random House.

Kristeva, Julia. 1982. *Powers of Horror.* New York: Columbia University Press.

Krupat, Arnold. 1989. *The Voice in the Margin: Native American Literature and the Canon.* Berkeley: University of California Press.

Kugelmass, Jack. 1980. *Native Aliens: The Jews of Poland as a Middleman Minority.* Ph.D. dissertation. New School for Social Research.

_____. 1986. *The Miracle of Intervale Avenue.* New York: Schocken.

_____, ed. 1988. *Between Two Worlds: Ethnographic Essays on American Jews.* Ithaca, N.Y.: Cornell University Press.

Kugelmass, Jack, and Jonathan Boyarin. 1983. *From a Ruined Garden: The Memorial Books of Polish Jewry.* New York: Schocken.

_____. 1988. "*Yizker Bikher* and the Problem of Historical Veracity: An Anthropological Approach." In *The Jews of Poland Between Two World Wars,* ed. Yisrael Gutman, Ezra Mendelsohn, Jehuda Reinharz, and Chone Shmeruk, 519-36. Hanover, N.H.: University Press of New England.

Lacoue-Labarthe, Philippe, and Jean-Luc Nancy. 1989. "The Nazi Myth." *Critical Inquiry* 16:291-312.

Lakoff, George, and Mark Johnson. 1980. *Metaphors We Live By.* Chicago: University of Chicago Press.

Lang, Berel. 1985. "Writing-the-holocaust: Jabès and the Measure of History." In *Edmond Jabès: The Sin of the Book,* ed. Eric Gould, 191-206. Lincoln: University of Nebraska Press.

Lapierre, Nicole. 1989. *Le Silence de la mémoire: A la recherche des juifs de Plock.* Paris: Plon.

Lefort, Claude. 1986. *Essais sur le politique.* Paris: Le Seuil.

Lentricchia, Frank. 1988. "Andiamo." *Critical Inquiry* 14:407-13.

Lévinas, Emmanuel. 1989. "Reflections on the Philosophy of Hitlerism." *Critical Inquiry* 17:62-71.

Levy, Benny. 1980. "Today's Hope: Conversations with Sartre." *Telos* 44 (Summer):155-80.

Lifton, Robert Jay. 1983. *The Broken Connection: On Death and the Continuity of Life.* New York: Basic Books.

Lloyd, David. 1987. "Genet's Genealogy: European Minorities and the Ends of the Canon." *Cultural Critique* 6:161-85.

———. 1989. "Kant's Examples." *Representations* 28:34-54.

Lloyd, Genevieve. 1985. *The Man of Reason: "Male" and "Female" in Western Philosophy.* Minneapolis: University of Minnesota Press.

Loefgren, Orvar. 1987. "Colonizing the Territory of Historical Anthropology." *Culture and History* 1:7-30.

Loewy, Michael. 1985. "Revolution Against Progress: Walter Benjamin's Romantic Anarchism." *New Left Review* 152:42-59.

Lyotard, Jean-François. 1984. *The Postmodern Condition: A Report on Knowledge.* Trans. Geoff Bennington and Brian Massumi. Minneapolis: University of Minnesota Press.

———. 1988. *The Differend: Phrases in Dispute.* Trans. Georges Van Den Abbeele. Minneapolis: University of Minnesota Press.

———. 1990. *Heidegger and "the jews."* Trans. Andreas Michel and Mark S. Roberts. Introd. by David Carroll. Minneapolis: University of Minnesota Press.

McHale, Brian. 1990. "Seizing the Means of Representation." *American Book Review* 11(6):4ff.

MacKinnon, Catherine A. 1982. "Feminism, Marxism, Method and the State: An Agenda for Theory." *Signs* 7:515-44.

———. 1988. "Desire and Power: A Feminist Perspective." In *Marxism and the Interpretation of Cultures,* ed. Cary Nelson and Lawrence Grossberg, 105-16. Urbana and Chicago: University of Illinois Press.

Marienstras, Richard. 1975. *Etre un peuple en diaspora.* Paris: Maspero.

Markish, Peretz. 1964. "Brokhshtiker" (Fragments). In *A shpigl oyf a shteyn,* ed. Chone Shmeruk, 489. Tel-Aviv: Farlag Di Goldene Keyt Un Y.L. Perets Farlag.

Markovits, Andrei S., and Rebecca S. Hayden. 1980. " 'Holocaust' Before and After the Event: Reactions in West Germany and Austria." *New German Critique* 19:53-80.

Marks, Elaine. Forthcoming. "Cendres Juives: Jews Writing in French After Auschwitz." In *Auschwitz and After: Jewish Culture in French Thought,* ed. Lawrence Kritzman.

Mascia-Lees, Frances E., Patricia Sharpe, and Colleen Ballerino Cohen. 1989. "The Postmodernist Turn in Anthropology: Some Cautions from a Feminist Perspective." *Signs* 15(1):7-33.

Mason, Peter. 1987. "Seduction from Afar: Europe's Inner Indians." *Anthropos* 82:581-601.

———. 1990. *Deconstructing America.* New York: Routledge.

May, Karl. 1979. *Winnetou.* Trans. Michael Shaw. New York: Seabury.

Memmi, Albert. 1967. *The Colonizer and the Colonized.* Boston: Beacon.

Mendelsohn, Ezra. 1970. *Class Struggle in the Pale.* Cambridge: Cambridge University Press.

Mitchell, Lee Clark. 1987. *Witnesses to a Vanishing America: The Nineteenth-Century Response.* Princeton, N.J.: Princeton University Press.

Modiano, Patrick. 1968. *La Place de l'étoile.* Paris: Gallimard.

Mohanty, S. P. 1989. "Us and Them: On the Philosophical Bases of Political Criticism." *Yale Journal of Criticism* 2(2):1-32.

Moore, Stephen D. 1989. *Literary Criticism and the Gospels: The Theoretical Challenge.* New Haven, Conn.: Yale University Press.

Morin, Edgar. 1971. *Rumour in Orleans.* New York: Pantheon.

Morrison, Karl F. 1988. *I Am You: The Hermeneutics of Empathy in Western Literature, Theology, and Art.* Princeton, N.J.: Princeton University Press.

Mosès, Stéphane. 1989. "The Theological-Political Model of History in the Thought of Walter Benjamin." *History and Memory* 1(2):5-34.

Mosse, George. 1985. *Nationalism and Sexuality.* Madison: University of Wisconsin Press.

Motte, Warren. 1990. *Questioning Edmond Jabès.* Lincoln: University of Nebraska Press.

Moughrabi, Fouad. 1989. "Redefining the Past." *Radical History Review* 45 (Fall):63-84.

Murdock, George Peter. 1961 [1953]. "The Processing of Anthropological Materials." In *Readings in Cross-Cultural Methodology*, ed. Frank W. Moore, 265-76. New Haven, Conn.: Human Relations Area Files Press.

Myerhoff, Barbara. 1978. *Number Our Days.* New York: Simon & Schuster.

New, Elisa. 1988. "Pharoah's Birthstool: Deconstruction and Midrash." *SubStance* 57:26-36.

Nora, Pierre, ed. 1984. *Les Lieux de mémoire.* Paris: Gallimard.

———. 1989. "Between Memory and History: *Les Lieux de mémoire.*" *Representations* 26:7-25.

Ohnuki-Tierney, Emiko, ed. 1990. *Culture through Time: Anthropological Approaches.* Stanford, Calif.: Stanford University Press.

Olender, Maurice. 1989. *Les langues du paradis: Aryens et Semites: un couple providentiel.* Paris: Gallimard and Le Seuil.

Pagels, Elaine. 1988. *Adam, Eve and the Serpent.* New York: Harper and Row.

Pearce, Roy Harvey. 1988 [1953]. *Savagism and Civilization: The Indian and the American Mind.* Berkeley: University of California Press.

Peled, Yoav. 1989. *Class and Ethnicity in the Pale: The Political Economy of Jewish Workers' Nationalism in Late Imperial Russia.* New York: St. Martin's.

Portugali, Yuval. 1988. "Nationalism, Social Theory and the Israeli/Palestinian Case." In *Nationalism, Self-Determination and Political Geography*, R. J. Johnston, David Knight, and Eleonore Kofman, eds., 151-65. London: Croon Helm.

Prakash, Gyan. 1990. "Writing Post-orientalist Histories of the Third World: Perspectives from Indian Historiography." *Comparative Studies in Society and History* 32:383-408.

Prince, Gerald. 1906. "Re-membering Modiano, or, Something Happened." *SubStance* 49:35-43.

Rabi, Wladimir. 1979. *Un Peuple de trop sur la terre?* Paris: Presses D'Aujourd'hui.

Rajchman, John. 1989. "Crisis." *Representations* 28:90-98.

Ratzel, Friedrich. 1898. *The History of Mankind* vol. 3. London and New York: Macmillan.

———. 1966. *Der Lebensraum: Ein biogeographische Studie.* Darmstadt: Wissenschaftliche Buchgesselschaft.

Rekhtman, Avrom. 1958. *Yidishe etnografye un folklor: zikhroynes vegn der etnografisher ekspeditsye ongefirt fun sh. anski.* Buenos Aires: Yidisher Visnshaftlekher Institute.

Rich, Adrienne. 1978. *The Dream of a Common Language: Poems 1974-1977.* New York: Norton.

Rolleston, James. 1989. "The Politics of Quotation: Walter Benjamin's Arcades Project." *Publications of the Modern Language Association* 104:13-27.

Ronell, Avital. 1989. "The Differends of Man." *Diacritics* 19(3-4):25-37.

Rosaldo, Renato. 1989. *Culture and Truth.* Boston: Beacon.

Said, Edward. 1978. *Orientalism.* New York: Pantheon.

_____. 1985. "Orientalism Reconsidered." *Cultural Critique* 1:89–107.

_____. 1986. *After the Last Sky: Palestinian Lives.* New York: Pantheon.

_____. 1989a. "*Intifada* and Independence." *Social Text* 22 (Spring):23–39.

_____. 1989b. "Representing the Colonized: Anthropology's Interlocutors." *Critical Inquiry* 15(2):205–25.

_____. 1989c. "Yeats and Decolonization." In *Remaking History*, ed. Barbara Kruger and Phil Mariani, 3–29. Seattle: Bay Press.

_____. 1989d. "Response." *Critical Inquiry* 15(3):634–46.

Scholem, Gershom. 1971. *The Messianic Idea in Judaism.* New York: Schocken.

Schor, Naomi. 1989. "This Essentialism Which Is Not One: Coming to Grips with Irigaray." *Differences* 1:38–58.

Schroyer, Trent. 1973. *The Critique of Domination.* New York: Beacon.

Sedgwick, Eve Kosofsky. 1985. *Between Men: English Literature and Male Homosocial Desire.* New York: Columbia University Press.

Shammas, Anton. 1986. *Arabesques.* New York: Harper and Row.

Shavit, Yaacov. 1990. "Cyrus King of Persia and the Return to Zion: A Case of Neglected Memory." *History and Memory* 2(1):51–83.

Shehadeh, Raja. 1984. *Samed: A Journal of Life on the West Bank.* New York: Adama.

Shell, Marc. 1988. *The End of Kinship: "Measure for Measure," Incest, and the Ideal of Universal Siblinghood.* Stanford, Calif.: Stanford University Press.

_____. 1991. "Marranos (Pigs); or, From Coexistence to Toleration." *Critical Inquiry* 17:306–35.

Shokeid, Moshe. 1988. "'The Manchester School in Africa and Israel" Revisited: Reflections on the Sources and Method of an Anthropological Discourse. *Israel Social Science Research* 6(1):9–23.

Smalley, Beryl. 1964. *The Study of the Bible in the Middle Ages.* South Bend, Ind.: University of Notre Dame Press.

Smith, Henry Nash. 1970 [1950]. *Virgin Land.* Cambridge, Mass.: Harvard University Press.

Soja, John. 1989. *Postmodern Geographies: The Reassertion of Space in Critical Social Theory.* London: Verso.

Sonnenfeld, Albert. 1989. "Swann's Nose." Lecture. Modern Language Association, Washington, D.C.

Spanos, William V. 1990. "Heidegger, Nazism, and the Repressive Hypothesis: The American Appropriation of the Question." *Boundary 2* 17(2):199–281.

Spivak, Gayatri Chakravorti. 1987. *In Other Worlds: Essays in Cultural Politics.* New York: Methuen.

_____. 1988. "Can the Subaltern Speak?" In *Marxism and the Interpretation of Culture*, ed. Cary Nelson and Lawrence Grossberg, 271–313. Urbana and Chicago: University of Illinois Press.

_____. 1989. "Who Claims Alterity?" In *Remaking History*, ed. Barbara Kruger and Phil Mariani, 269–92. Seattle: Bay Press.

_____. 1990. *The Post-Colonial Critic.* Interviews. Ed. Sarah Harasym. New York: Routledge.

Taussig, Michael. 1984. "Culture of Terror, Space of Death: Roger Casement's Putumayo Report and the Explanation of Torture." *Comparative Studies in Society and History* 26:467–97.

_____. 1987. *Shamanism, Colonialism, and the Wild Man: A Study in Terror and Healing.* Chicago: Chicago University Press.

Taylor, Charles. 1990. "Modes of Civil Society." *Public Culture* 3 (Fall):95–118.

Theweleit, Klaus. 1987. *Male Fantasies. Vol. 1: Women, Floods, Bodies, History.* Minneapolis: University of Minnesota Press.

———. 1989. *Male Fantasies. Vol. 2: Male Bodies: Psychoanalyzing the White Terror.* Minneapolis: University of Minnesota Press.

Thom, Martin. 1990. "Tribes Within Nations: The Ancient Germans and the History of Modern France." In *Nation and Narration*, ed. Homi K. Bhabha, 23–43. New York: Routledge.

Thornton, Robert. 1988. "The Rhetoric of Ethnographic Holism." *Cultural Anthropology* 3(3):285–303.

Todorov, Tristan. 1985. *The Conquest of America: The Question of the Other.* New York: Harper and Row.

Torgovnick, Marianna. 1990. *Gone Primitive: Savage Intellects, Modern Lives.* Chicago: University of Chicago Press.

Tuan, Yi-Fu. 1974. *Topophilia.* Englewood Cliffs, N.J.: Prentice-Hall.

Turner, Frederick W. 1980. *Beyond Geography.* New Brunswick, N.J.: Rutgers University Press.

Tyler, Stephen. 1987. *The Unspeakable.* Madison: University of Wisconsin Press.

Vagts, Alfred. 1957. "The Germans and the Red Man." *American-German Review* 24:13–17.

van Gennep, A. 1920. "Nouvelles recherches sur l'histoire en France de la méthode ethnographique: Claude Guichard, Richard Simon, Claude Fleury." *Revue de l'histoire des religions* 82–83:139–62.

van Teeffelen, T. 1978. "The Manchester School in Africa and Israel." *Dialectical Anthropology* 3(1):67–84.

Varenne, Hervè. 1986. "Drop in Anytime: Community and Authenticity in American Life." In *Symbolizing America*, ed. Hervè Varenne, 209–28. Lincoln: University of Nebraska Press.

Vidal-Nacquet, Pierre. 1982. "Herodote et l'Atlantide: entre les Grecs et les Juifs. Reflexions sur l'historiographie du siècle des Lumieres." *Quaderni Di Storia* 16:5–74.

Vizenor, Gerald. 1988. *The Trickster of Liberty: Tribal Heirs to a Wild Baronage.* Minneapolis: University of Minnesota Press.

———. 1989. "A Postmodern Introduction." In *Narrative Chance: Postmodern Discourse on Native American Indian Literatures*, ed. Gerald Vizenor, 3–16. Albuquerque: University of New Mexico Press.

Wasserman, Suzanne. 1987. "Shvitzing, Shpritzing and Fressing: A Critical Look at Memories of the 'Good Old Days' on the Lower East Side." Paper presented at YIVO Conference on Authenticity and Nostalgia, New York City.

Weinreich, Max. 1980. *The History of the Yiddish Language.* Chicago: University of Chicago Press.

Wertheimer, Jack. 1987. *Unwelcome Strangers: East European Jews in Imperial Germany.* New York: Oxford University Press.

Wissler, Clark. 1950. *The American Indian.* New York: Peter Smith.

Wolin, Richard. 1982. *Walter Benjamin: An Aesthetics of Redemption.* New York: Columbia University Press.

Wood, Bryce. 1968. "Area Studies." In *International Encyclopedia of the Social Sciences*, Vol. 1. New York: Macmillan and Free Press.

Yardeni, Myriam. 1970. "La Vision des juifs et du judaisme dans l'oeuvre de Richard Simon." *Revue des etudes juives* 129:179–203.

Yerushalmi, Yosef Haim. 1982. *Zakhor: Jewish History and Jewish Memory*. Seattle: University of Washington Press.

_____. 1988. "Réflexions sur l'oubli." In *Les Usages de l'oubli*, 7-21. Paris: Le Seuil.

Young, James E. 1989. "The Biography of a Memorial Icon: Nathan Rapoport's Warsaw Ghetto Monument." *Representations* 26:69-106.

Zborowski, Mark, and Elizabeth Herzog. 1976 [1952]. *Life Is with People*. New York: Schocken.

Zhitlovsky, Chaim. 1912. *Tsvey forlezungen vegn yid un mensh*. New York: Zhitlovsky Jubilee Committee.

Zielinski, Siefried. 1980. "History as Entertainment and Provocation: The TV Series 'Holocaust' in West Germany." *New German Critique* 19:81-96.

Index

Jonathan Boyarin is currently Visiting Scholar at the Center for Studies of Social Change at the New School for Social Research, where he is researching the cultural construction of Israeli and Palestinian nationalisms. He is the author of *Polish Jews in Paris: The Ethnography of Memory* (1991) and *From a Ruined Garden* (1983) and has published numerous articles on the politics of ethnography and cultural histories.

$39.95